The Perfect Ingredient

Bryn Williams

One of the greatest joys of food is
the sharing of it. Sharing a table with
Sharleen and Misty is *my* greatest joy.

The Perfect Ingredient

5 fantastic ways to cook
apples, beets, pork, scallops and more

Bryn Williams

with Kay Plunkett-Hogge

Photographs by Jonathan Gregson

Kyle Books

Published in 2012 by Kyle Books,
an imprint of Kyle Cathie Limited.
www.kylebooks.com

Distributed by National Book Network
4501 Forbes Blvd., Suite 200
Lanham, MD 20706
Phone: (800) 462-6420
Fax: (301) 429-5746
custserv@nbnbooks.com

First published in Great Britain in 2011 by
Kyle Books Limited.

10 9 8 7 6 5 4 3 2 1

ISBN: 978-1-906868-49-9

Project Editor: Jenny Wheatley
Art Direction & Design: Aboud Creative
Photographer: Jonathan Gregson
Home Economist: Annie Rigg
Stylist: Liz Belton
Americanizer: Margaret Parrish
Production: Sheila Smith and Nic Jones

Library of Congress Control Number:
2011940445

Color reproduction by Sang Choy
in Singapore.

Printed in China by C&C Offset
Printing Co., Ltd.

Contents

Introduction

When I was a boy, I used to earn pocket money by picking potatoes on my uncle's farm and packing them in burlap sacks. We were paid by weight. Now that I'm an adult, I can finally admit to something: this was such hard, backbreaking work that, by dusk, I'd accumulated a fair number of stones in my sack to make up the pounds. To this day, I blush at the thought. But I did pick potatoes. I did see how incredibly hard people work to produce the food on our plates. That's what drives me in my work today. And it was with this thought very much in mind that I decided to write this book—to share my conviction that all food should have our utmost respect, even the humble spud.

Each chapter in this book showcases an ingredient or food that I love. I have room here for only 20, but every one is a perfect product of nature and nurture. And for each one I have listed five methods of cooking, from the very simplest ways to some of the more complex, "cheffy" recipes I have developed on my journey from the heart of Wales to my restaurant, Odette's, in Primrose Hill, London.

The goal in writing this book is not to promote me as a chef; it's all about the ingredients. The recipes are just blueprints to inspire you to cook, and to build on your own cooking skills. I am simply here to guide you, suggesting interesting flavor combinations, some new cuts of meat, and maybe a vegetable or two that you might have overlooked.

I believe that we need to look to the land from which our food comes—and to look after it. If you abuse a field this year, you sure as hell aren't getting any crops from it next year. Overfish this year? No fish the next. And so it goes with hunting and animal husbandry, too. What can we do to respect the land, the ocean, and the animals that give us our food? Use as much of the animal, fish, or crop as we can. Explore beyond the usual cuts, looking at what else the butcher has in stock. Ask friends and family what they use. Buy as seasonally as possible. Make stocks to catch and use up every last bit of flavor. Try baking bread at home just to taste the difference.

I'm a great believer, too, in cooking from the heart and soul. If there's a missing ingredient in a dish, it could be love! I really do believe that. And in the sharing of food. What's the point of choosing ingredients, creating a dish, and setting a beautiful table if you have no one to share your food with?

I remember my first attempt at cooking. I stood on a stool in my Mam's kitchen and made a chocolate cornflake cake. And it wasn't great just because it tasted fantastic (although, thinking about it, maybe that should go back on the menu...); it was great because I'd made it, and Mam and I could share it.

My family is very important to me—they have shaped my thoughts on our responsibility to the land and on good food. Every year, the whole clan gathers to celebrate Nain's birthday (that's Welsh for Granny): fourteen uncles and aunts, 20 grandchildren with husbands and wives, and numerous great-grandchildren. A couple of years ago we held a grand picnic at a park not far from the farm. Every family member brought a different dish. Under an awning we set up a trestle table groaning with homemade goodies, and as soon as Nain had taken her first helping, everyone else plowed in. Children played cricket or paddled boats on a pond nearby. And then my Uncle John noticed that an American couple and their two children had joined the line for food. They piled their plates high and then inquired where they should pay. My father turned to them and said, "You don't pay. This is a celebration. Help yourselves. Join us." So the family of four Americans joined us and celebrated, too. That's the way food should be eaten. And that's what I want to convey in this book: that your family and friends deserve the best you can give them.

In Welsh we have a word—*hiraeth*. It describes a feeling of belonging—to a place, to a person. It's where you are from, it's what you're about. We are all caretakers of the land we live off. We can all do our bit *and* eat very well out of it. So whether you are trawling the supermarket aisles or have the opportunity—and please, please take it if you do—to use farmers' markets, butchers, greengrocers, and fishmongers, choose the best ingredients you can afford. Enjoy preparing and cooking them. And, most of all, savor the pleasure of eating and sharing something you have created yourself.

Recipe Key

The recipes in each chapter range from easy to complex— look for the following symbols:

Easy

Medium

Complex

Useful Equipment

I thought it would be a good idea to introduce the five items I think you really can't do without in a kitchen. You don't need a lot of complex gadgets to cook well, and none of those mentioned here will break the bank. What these five simple items will do is make your life in the kitchen easier and more enjoyable.

Good Knives

Knives that maintain a sharp edge are vital—and not only for the obvious uses in chopping, slicing, and cutting. Most importantly, a sharp knife is more predictable than a blunt one, and less likely to glance off whatever you are chopping and into your hand. If you do manage to cut yourself—and let's face it, who doesn't?—a cut from a sharp blade will be easier to clean and will heal better than a jagged gash from a blunt knife. It also hurts less.

You really need only three knives—a good carving knife, a big-bladed chef's knife for chopping and slicing, and a paring knife. You will also need a good steel to keep a sharp edge on the blades. Or, if you prefer, you could use a knife-sharpening service—available at some kitchenware stores or by mail—since maintaining your knives year by year is much more cost-effective than buying new ones.

Fine Strainer

Chefs call a fine, cone-shaped strainer a "chinois." Using one is a simple way to give soups and sauces a smooth, professional touch. I use them all the time. If you get in the habit of using a fine strainer regularly, you'll notice a difference in your dishes. It's the kind of attention to detail that just raises everything up. After all, a clean silky sauce or custard looks and feels so much better than one with misplaced lumps in it.

Sturdy Pans

You don't need a huge number of pans, just a few solid basics. The first essential is a sturdy, heavy-bottomed, metal-handled sauté or frying pan that can go straight from the stove into the oven. You just have to remember that the handle will get hot!

A wide, deep baking dish with a good-fitting lid is another must—again, one that can go directly from stove to oven is best. And, of course, you need a couple of saucepans, one of which should be large enough to make a decent 2 quarts of stock. Finally, find a good-quality nonstick frying pan for cooking fish and omelets.

Food processor

By this, I mean, for example, a Kenwood or Magimix food processor or a Kitchen Aid stand mixer that can chop, slice, and dice, but also blend pastry and liquidize. Ideally, it should have changeable parts so that you can put on the dough hook for bread-making and then quickly and easily change the attachment to beat egg whites to peaks. There are so many models to choose from that you are sure to find one that fits your budget and kitchen space.

Blender

To blend soups and purées and liquidize drinks and sauces, I recommend either a standard worktop electric blender or a small handheld immersion blender. Again, they are available at a price to suit every budget.

dwarter o ...ne acd, a chwarter pwys o cymfferm,
neu flawd rhygyn ... en hidlo ddwy waith.
Gadaer i'r y cyfan o'r defnyddiau yn herfaith sych,
a llw'r gymmysger hwynt trwy en hidlo ddwy waith.

BARA BARU (*Bara Loff*).—Dau bwys o flawd, pwys o sugr mân,
hanner pwys o ryfon, chwarter
pwys o flonog, pwys a hanner ... sych, fws-
ate o soda, ac ychydig grisialedig. honaid llwy dâ o carbon-
lin, rhodder y sugr grisialedig lai o *tartaric acid*, a llaeth enwyn.
ol ei datellu i'r blawd, hidler y powdr trwy fws-
llaeth enwyn yn does ysgafn, a llaeth enwyn
pobty enwyn yn fan, ynddo, a chymmysger y cyfan mewn
dorth ganolig o faint. Gwna yr uchod ddwy

BARA CEIRCH (*Oat Cake*).—Cymmysger blawd ceirch gyda dwfr berwedig yn lled
dew; rholier ef allan yn denen a chrwn, a chraser ar
radell am ychydig funydau. Sycher o flaen y tân nes
yn galed.

BARA HADAU (*Seed Bread*).—Dau bwys o flawd, chwarter pwys o gigferion glân, chwe wns o sugr coch, hanner wns o hadau
caraway, ac ychydig furym. Cymmysger y sugr a'r hadau gyda'r
cigferion mewn dwfr cynnes, a defnyddier ei gymmysgu
yn ddwy dorth i'w crasu mewn tins.

BARA RHYFON (*Currant Bread*).—Dau bwys o flawd, tri chwarter pwys o
ryfon, chwarter pwys o gigferion wedi ei dori yn fan, ac wns
o groen suryn grisialedig, ac o sugr coch, dwy
o furym. Cymmysger y rhyfon, sugr, a chroen suryn grisialedig gyda'r blawd; gosoder heples o'r burym wedi ei

Beets

Both my father and my uncle swore that they could tell which field on the farm a beet came from by taste alone. The French, I suppose, would think of this as *terroir*: a connection with the soil and with a place.

One of my earliest memories is an image of my uncle's weather-worn hands holding a bunch of freshly pulled beets, their leaves thick and glossy, their roots covered with rich soil. And I can't escape the thought that the earth of the farm at Llanrhaeadr is a part of him, of me, and of my family, that we are bound somehow to that piece of land. The beets we grew weren't just for us, though. They were reliable, cheap food for the pigs as well. And they were delicious. Along with some crisp apples, fresh milk from the dairy, and a few slices of home-cured ham, they became a staple snack on many an afternoon fishing trip.

I love beets. I know they're not glamorous and that they're a bit unfashionable—you don't really see them on many menus—but I think they're beautiful. It's not just the color, which can range from ruby red to gold to the candy beet, with its red and white swirls; it's the bright, sweet, nutty flavor. It's such a shame that so many people, when they think of beets, remember only the horrible vinegar-saturated things they were made to eat as kids. There's so much more to beets than that. Beets mash and purée fantastically, adding color and life to the plate. They have a natural affinity for game in all its guises.

Baby beets have a different feel and taste from the larger roots. The young shoots are great for salads, contributing color and sweetness. Even raw, beets have an earthy, sweet-sour quality all their own. When you're buying these root vegetables, look for firm, almost hard beets with perky leaves to be sure you take home maximum flavor.

I suppose that some people, when they cook with beets, might worry that they'll end up with beet-red fingers after handling them. Well, that is a risk. To combat it, just wear disposable gloves, or lightly coat your hands in vegetable oil—not too much though, since you don't want the beets shooting from your grasp, but just enough so that the juices don't leave their mark.

Beyond the taste, beets are good for our environment, too. They are good value. They don't need a lot of pesticide. They've got a long growing season. And they also pickle well, making them something of a year-round staple. They are, I think, roots we should learn to love in all their forms.

Caramelized Beets

Simple, caramelized chunks of sweet beets are excellent with game and red meat. You could use them as a substitute for the red cabbage in the Roast Mallard dish on page 167, or with the Roast Rib-eye steak on page 129.

Preheat the oven to 325°F.

Wrap the beets individually in foil and place them on a roasting pan lined with rock salt. This helps to draw out moisture, even when the beets are wrapped in foil. Bake in the oven for 2 hours.

Remove the beets from the oven and set aside to cool in the foil—they will steam a little, which makes them easier to peel. Save the rock salt to use again.

When the beets are cool, peel them and cut them in half. Season with a pinch of salt and the sugar.

Place a heavy-bottomed frying pan over medium heat. Add the vegetable oil. When it is hot, place the beet halves in the pan flat-side down, add the thyme and garlic, and leave until the beets turn golden brown and are caramelized. Turn the beets over, remove from the pan, and serve at once.

Serves 4

2 large beets

about ¾ cup rock salt

pinch of salt

1 tsp sugar

1 tbsp vegetable oil

sprig of thyme

3–4 garlic cloves, unpeeled

BRYN'S TIPS

Baking on salt is an effective way to draw out excess moisture. I prefer rock salt, but feel free to use any type of salt you like. And remember, you can reuse the salt afterward.

Beet Purée

Serves 4–6

¾lb beets

about ¾ cup rock salt

½ cup superfine sugar

¼ cup port

¼ cup apple juice

I love to serve this with an oily fish, such as salmon or mackerel. It lifts the flavor and counteracts the richness, while adding a dramatic flash of color to the plate. The purée is best served at room temperature.

Preheat the oven to 350°F.

Wrap the beets individually in foil and place them on a roasting pan lined with rock salt. This helps to draw out moisture, even when the beets are wrapped in foil. Bake in the oven for 2½–3 hours, or until very soft.

Remove the beets from the oven and set aside to cool in the foil—they will steam a little, which makes them easier to peel. Save the salt to use again.

When they are cool, peel the beets and cut them into small cubes.

Put the diced beets in a saucepan and add the sugar, port, and apple juice. Bring to a boil until the sugar is just dissolved, then pour everything into a blender or food processor and blend until smooth. Remember, the mixture will be hot, so take care. Pass through a fine strainer and set aside until needed.

Beet Gratin

This is a lovely take on a dauphinoise. The beets add a sweet nuttiness, while the potatoes provide much-needed starch to absorb the cream, making this a rich and delicious dish. It goes beautifully with game; I often pair it with the Peppered Loin of Venison on page 164. But you could serve it as a vegetarian main course, too.

Preheat the oven to 325°F.

In a heavy-bottomed saucepan, bring the cream, milk, thyme, peppercorns, and garlic to a boil. Immediately remove from the heat and set aside to infuse.

Season the buttered gratin dish with salt and pepper. Arrange the slices of beets and potato in the dish, overlapping them and seasoning each layer as you go.

Strain the cream mixture through a fine strainer, then pour it over the dish, making sure the vegetables are well covered. Bake in the oven for 45–55 minutes, until the potatoes and beets are cooked and have absorbed the cream. Check whether the vegetables are done by poking the layers with a knife; they should give nicely.

Serves 4–6 as a side dish

1⅔ cups heavy cream

⅓ cup milk

sprig of thyme

4 black peppercorns

2 garlic cloves, peeled and crushed

salt and pepper

10oz beets, peeled and thinly sliced

7oz potatoes, peeled and thinly sliced

You will need a well-buttered 10in gratin dish.

Beet Soup

Serves 4

2 tbsp olive oil

1 onion, peeled and sliced

8 large beets, peeled and diced

1 quart Vegetable Stock (see page 257)

12 baby beets, unpeeled

salt and pepper

sprig of thyme

½ cup crème fraîche

Rich, ruby-red, and sweet—thanks to the roasted baby beets—this is one of my absolute favorite soups. It captures everything I love about this vegetable.

Preheat the oven to 325°F.

Heat the olive oil in a heavy-bottomed saucepan. Add the onion and cook until soft. Add the diced beets to the onion and cook for 2–3 minutes. Pour in the vegetable stock, bring to a boil, and simmer for 15 minutes.

While the soup is cooking, place the baby beets in a roasting pan and season well with salt, pepper, and the sprig of thyme. Roast in the oven for 10–15 minutes, until soft. When the beets are done, peel off the outer skin—it should simply slip off—and set aside.

When the soup is ready, pour into a blender or food processor and blend until smooth. Remember, it will be very hot, so be careful. Pass the soup through a fine strainer, pour it back into a clean saucepan, and keep hot over low heat.

To serve, divide the roasted baby beets into four bowls. Pour the soup over the top and finish with a spoonful of the crème fraîche.

Beet Tarte Tatin

I love a tarte tatin and felt that beets would work well cooked this way. This is great as an appetizer, but I also like to serve it with a cheese course. It goes beautifully with goat cheese and a drizzle of good-quality honey.

Preheat the oven to 350°F.

Wrap the beets individually in foil and place them on a roasting pan lined with rock salt. This helps to draw out moisture, even when the beets are wrapped in foil. Bake in the oven for 1½ hours.

Remove the beets from the oven and set aside to cool in the foil—they will steam a little, which makes them easier to peel. Save the salt to use again. When they are cool, peel the beets, cut them into quarters, and set aside.

Cover the bottom of the frying pan evenly with the butter—use your fingers, really squashing the butter down. Then sprinkle the sugar evenly over the butter. Place the pan over medium heat until the butter melts and the sugar starts turning a light golden color. Now place the beet quarters on top, arranging them in concentric circles until they are all used up. Set aside to cool.

On a floured surface, roll out the puff pastry to a thickness of ⅛in. Pay attention to the size as you are rolling: the pastry must be big enough to cover the beets in the pan. Place the puff pastry gently over the top of the beets, tucking any excess pastry between the beets and the pan like a blanket. Brush the pastry with the beaten egg.

Put the tart in the oven for about 40 minutes, or until golden brown and oozing caramel slightly at the edges. Remove from the oven and turn onto a plate to serve.

Serves 4

3 large beets

about ¾ cup rock salt

5 tbsp unsalted butter, softened

⅓ cup superfine sugar

flour, for dusting

4oz puff pastry (ready-made is fine)

1 egg, lightly beaten

You will need an 8in shallow frying pan with a metal handle.

Mushrooms

When I was younger and we went hunting, there seemed to be wild mushrooms growing all over the place on my uncle's farm. Hundreds of them. We didn't pick them, mainly because we didn't know what they were—and here I'll slot in the advisory note. *Do not* pick wild mushrooms unless you have an expert knowledge of them and can identify the different types. If you *really* want to pick them, make sure you find an expert to go with you. Mushroom poisoning is not something to take lightly. Now, if only I'd been an expert back then! I'm pretty sure there would have been porcinis and chanterelles galore. Both grow in Wales during the game season—another example of the free food I often talk about, growing right there under our noses.

There are countless varieties of mushroom, wild and cultivated. Porcinis are meaty and substantial, and great for roasting; chanterelles and black trumpets are excellent for pasta and risottos, holding their shape even as they soften. But, as much as I love wild mushrooms, there's a great deal to be said for the underrated and ever-so-slightly unfashionable button and crimini mushrooms, too. They have a hell of a lot of flavor, sometimes more than pricey wild mushrooms, as do big, juicy field mushrooms.

Button and crimini mushrooms are great for soups, or quickly sautéed, for a midweek supper. For one of my absolute favorites, I quarter some button mushrooms, fry them in butter, drain them, add a dash of Worcestershire sauce and a bit of salt, and serve them with a juicy steak.

Dried mushrooms are chock full of flavor, too, and tend to be the ones gathered and preserved at the end of the harvest. They're a terrific pantry staple, ideal for adding depth and richness to your cooking. To bring them back to life, just pour warm water over them, allow them to plump up, and then drain.

I love the texture of mushrooms as well as the flavor, but they do have to be cooked properly. You must get all the water out. Water makes up about 90 percent of mushrooms, so you have to cook them in a hot pan until all the liquid comes out and then evaporates. Only then will you unlock that true musky, woodsy, meaty mushroom taste. And it's all too easy to add water to them by mistake, when you're cleaning them. Never leave mushrooms soaking in water; clean them quickly and gently. You can use a clean brush, dipped lightly in water, making sure you work the brush into the gills. With other mushrooms, put them in cold water and gently move them around, being careful not to damage them, then drain at once. (You may need to do this a couple of times if they are really dirty.) Dry them thoroughly with paper towels before cooking them. With some of the woodier or bigger mushrooms, such as chanterelles, you can scrape their stalks, too, or it may be easier to peel the dirt and the skin off them in one. Don't forget—keep all the trimmings for the stock on page 256.

Most of the dishes in this chapter are vegetarian. Mushrooms provide a chunky, substantial alternative for the non-meat-eater, and meat fans love them, too. What a win-win ingredient!

Wild Mushrooms on Toast

Serves 4

2 tbsp butter, plus extra for spreading

10oz mixed wild mushrooms, trimmed, washed, and dried

salt and pepper

1 shallot, peeled and finely chopped

1 heaping tbsp wild garlic greens, finely chopped (see tip, below)

4 large slices of sourdough bread

handful of parsley, finely chopped

Although incredibly simple to make, this is not just delicious, but also impressive. Try to mix and match mushrooms for their differing textures and flavors. If you can't find wild mushrooms, use a selection of good old button, black poplar, crimini, and portobello. They all taste fantastic.

Melt the butter in a heavy-bottomed frying pan and, when it is hot, gently sauté the mushrooms until they start to soften. Season to taste with salt and pepper.

As the mushrooms cook, they will give off a lot of moisture. When all the liquid has evaporated, add the shallot to the pan and cook for a minute or so, until softened. Add the wild garlic, stir, and remove from the heat immediately. Set aside and keep warm.

Lightly toast the slices of sourdough bread, spread them with butter, and pile the mushrooms on top. Serve with chopped parsley scattered on top.

Bryn's Tips
This dish tastes terrific topped with a poached or fried egg.

If wild garlic is not in season, substitute 2 cloves of regular garlic, peeled and finely chopped, and some chopped fresh parsley.

Pan-fried Porcinis, Bacon, & Duck Egg

The porcini is the daddy of mushrooms: musky, earthy, meaty, and simply delicious. Here, porcinis are combined with creamy duck eggs, fresh herbs, and crisp, salty bacon to make a meal fit for a king. Serve for breakfast, lunch, or dinner—or any time in between.

Gently clean the porcinis in cold water one at a time, then set them aside to dry on paper towels.

In a large, heavy-bottomed frying pan, heat 1 tablespoon of the olive oil and brown the bacon, turning it occasionally, until it is golden and crispy. This should take 2–3 minutes. Remove the bacon from the pan, drain on paper towels, and set aside.

Cut the porcinis in half. Season to taste with salt and pepper. Add the remaining olive oil to the frying pan, heat it up, and then add the porcinis, flat-side down. Cook them for 2–3 minutes, until they are still firm, but have a little color. Then add the butter and the thyme, turn the porcinis over, and cook for another minute, until just cooked through. Add the bacon, set aside, and keep warm.

In another large frying pan, heat the vegetable oil and fry the duck eggs until they have a firm white and a runny yolk. Season with salt and pepper. Serve each duck egg with porcinis and bacon on the side.

Serves 4

8 medium porcini mushrooms

2 tbsp olive oil

4oz bacon

salt and pepper

2 tbsp butter

1 tbsp fresh thyme leaves

2 tbsp vegetable oil

4 duck eggs

Mushroom Risotto

Serves 4–6 as an appetizer

1 quart Mushroom Stock
(see page 256) or Chicken
Stock (see page 259),
or a mixture of both

¼ cup butter

2 tbsp olive oil

2 shallots, peeled and
finely chopped

1 cup risotto rice

⅓ cup white wine

salt and pepper

4oz wild mushrooms,
trimmed, washed,
dried, and quartered

½ cup finely grated
Parmesan, plus extra
for serving

1–2 tbsp chopped
flat-leaf parsley

Rich, creamy, just-cooked risotto marries so well with mushrooms and cheese—they were made to go together. Don't be afraid of risottos. I know they seem time-consuming, but they aren't if you are chatting and sipping a glass of wine while stirring and ladling stock.

Pour the stock into a saucepan and bring to a boil over medium heat. Keep on low heat within easy reach until needed.

Now, melt the butter with 1 tablespoon of the olive oil in a heavy-bottomed saucepan. Add the chopped shallots and cook for 2–3 minutes, or until soft. Add the rice, stir well to coat it with the butter and shallot mixture, then cook for another minute. Pour in the white wine, stirring continuously until all the liquid has been absorbed.

Add a ladleful of the simmering stock to the rice, stirring all the time, and cook until the stock has been absorbed before adding another ladleful. Repeat until the rice is tender but retains a little bite—this should take about 20 minutes. When the risotto is ready, season with salt and pepper. Then, remove from the heat, put on a lid, set aside, and keep warm.

Heat a heavy-bottomed frying pan and, once it is hot, add the remaining olive oil. Add the mushrooms and cook for 1–2 minutes, or until just soft. Spoon the mushrooms onto paper towels to absorb any excess oil.

Stir the Parmesan and parsley into the risotto. Add the mushrooms, stirring them in gently. If the risotto feels a little firm, stir through some stock before serving. Serve topped with freshly grated Parmesan.

Mushroom Soup

Serves 4–6

¼ cup butter

1 onion, peeled and sliced

sprig of thyme

8oz button mushrooms, trimmed, washed, dried, and sliced

salt and pepper

1½ cups Mushroom Stock (see page 256) or Chicken Stock (see page 259)

1½ cups heavy cream

Comforting, musky, rich, creamy—the joys of homemade mushroom soup. This recipe is so simple, too.

In a large, heavy-bottomed saucepan, melt the butter over low heat, without allowing it to color. Add the onion and the thyme, and let the onion break down gently for 4–5 minutes, or until soft. Add the sliced mushrooms and allow them to sweat for another 7–8 minutes, until all their water has evaporated. Season the mushroom mixture with salt and pepper to taste.

Add the stock to the saucepan and bring it to a boil. Simmer for 2–3 minutes, then add the cream. Bring back to a boil, then remove from the heat and blend with a hand blender until smooth. Alternatively, allow to cool a little, then blend in a blender or food processor.

Pass the soup through a fine strainer into a serving bowl and serve immediately.

BRYN'S TIPS
I like to garnish this soup with a few of the Pickled Mushrooms on page 246, but you could sauté a few wild mushrooms and scatter them on top.

It's important that you allow the mushrooms to sweat until all the water they release has evaporated; this will give the dish more flavor and a better color.

Mushroom Lasagne

This is one of the most popular vegetarian options on the menu at Odette's. The trick here is to allow enough preparation time.

First, make the pasta. In a large bowl, mix together the olive oil and the eggs. Place the flour and salt in a food processor and, with the motor running, slowly add the oil and egg mixture until the texture resembles fine bread crumbs. Then, using your hands, bring it together to create a dough that is firm to the touch and fairly dry. Depending on the size of the eggs, you may need to add 1 tablespoon water to help the dough come together. Place the pasta dough on a clean, lightly floured work surface and knead it for 3–5 minutes. Cut into three pieces and wrap them individually in plastic wrap. Place all three in the refrigerator to rest for at least 1 hour.

Set the pasta machine to its thickest setting and pass one piece of dough through the rollers. Change the setting to the next-thickest and pass the sheet through the machine again. Repeat, keeping each sheet as wide as the machine and reducing the thickness setting each time, until you have rolled the sheet through the thinnest setting. Repeat with the two remaining pieces of dough.

Cook the pasta sheets in a large saucepan of boiling salted water for 1 minute. Take them out immediately and place in a large bowl of iced water to prevent the pasta from overcooking. When it is cold, remove the pasta from the water and set aside to dry.

Preheat the oven to 300°F.

To make the filling, melt the butter in a large saucepan. Add the mushrooms and thyme and cook for 6–7 minutes, or until the mushrooms are cooked and all the liquid has evaporated. Season to taste. Remove half the mushrooms with a slotted spoon and set aside. Add the cream to the remaining mushrooms in the pan, bring to a boil, and simmer for 1 minute. Remove from the heat and allow to cool a little. Then, carefully—it will be hot—pour the mixture into a blender or food processor. Don't overfill the machine or it may splatter while blending. Add the agar-agar and blend to a smooth purée. Pour the mushroom purée into a large bowl. Add the set-aside mushrooms and mix well. Check the seasoning, then set aside, and keep warm.

To assemble the lasagne, line the bottom of the baking dish with one sheet of pasta. Spoon half of the warm mushroom filling on top and spread evenly. Cover with another sheet of pasta, then pour the remaining mushroom mixture on top. Spread evenly and finish off with the final sheet of pasta—sprinkle a little Parmesan on top, if you wish. Place in the oven for 10 minutes, to finish cooking the pasta, then remove from the oven, cut into portions, and serve.

Serves 4–6

For the pasta

1 tbsp olive oil

2 eggs

2½ cups "oo" flour, plus extra for dusting (see tip on page 46)

pinch of salt

For the filling

¼ cup butter

2lb button mushrooms, trimmed, washed, dried, and thinly sliced

1 tbsp fresh thyme leaves

salt and pepper

⅔ cup heavy cream

1 tbsp agar-agar (a vegetarian alternative to gelatin, derived from seaweed)

olive oil, for greasing

grated Parmesan, for sprinkling

You will need a pasta machine and a 9 × 10in baking dish, greased with olive oil.

Potatoes

As kids, my brothers and I would fight like cats and dogs. When we'd finally exhausted Mam's patience, she'd send us down to my uncle's farm for potatoes, just to get us out of the house. An hour or so later, we'd be back at her table eating them.

Of all the ingredients I've chosen for this book, potatoes seem to form the backbone of so many of my memories. I have planted them, picked them, sold them, and eaten them. They weren't just a part of almost every meal during my childhood, they were a part of the fabric of our lives. On the farm, we used to plant them according to the bell. My uncle would drive the tractor, with my dad and me sitting on the back as he hoed the ground. At fixed intervals, the bell would ring and we'd drop a seed potato into the soil. It's an old-fashioned technique, but it works, reminding you to space each plant evenly across the field. That way, you get as many as you can into the plot and give each one the room it needs to produce the maximum yield.

In the field, there was a flag to show the position of the older potatoes; the ones we'd harvest first. But I especially loved the new potatoes we earthed up in early summer. We used to call them marble potatoes, because of their size. My Dad has a special method of cleaning them: put the potatoes in a bucket with lots of water, grab a broom handle, and stir, stir, stir—the centrifugal force pulls off the dirt. But sometimes, in the field, he'd rub the skin off a potato on his pants and eat it raw, there and then!

My Gran used to boil potatoes, lightly crush them, then pour over buttermilk (which we always had because we made our own butter). She said to me recently, "Apparently, you can buy it in the supermarket now." The potatoes would absorb it all, and we'd eat them hot, dipped in salt. They were fantastic!

There are so many different varieties of potato that it's sometimes difficult to know which one to use in a particular recipe. All of them have their uses for certain dishes. All-Blue and Yellow Finn—both varieties are best as new potatoes— are quite firm and waxy, and great simply boiled or used in salads. I prefer Desirée for mashing and baking, while Russet and Bintje potatoes are great for roasting and fries. It is very important to use the right potato for the right job! I recommend Desirée in all the recipes in this chapter—but if you cannot find them, Russet or any other floury potato should work.

Leek & Potato Soup

Serves 4–6 as an appetizer

1 quart Vegetable Stock
(see page 257) or Chicken
Stock (see page 259)

½ cup butter

1 onion, peeled and sliced

2 leeks, washed and sliced,
with the white and green
parts kept separate

salt and pepper

1 large Desirée or
Russet potato, peeled
and very thinly sliced

As a Welshman, I just had to feature leeks in the book. This is a beautifully creamy soup—containing not a drop of cream! I like to serve it topped with some finely diced fried potatoes and cooked leeks.

Pour the stock into a saucepan and bring to a boil over medium heat. Reduce to a simmer and keep within easy reach until needed.

In a large, heavy-bottomed saucepan, melt the butter, without allowing it to color. Add the onion and cook until soft. Add the white part of the leeks and cook for 2 minutes longer, again, not allowing anything to color. Season to taste with salt and pepper. Add the potato and the green part of the leeks, and stir well.

Now pour the hot stock over the top and let everything boil for 2–3 minutes, or until the potato is cooked through. Remove from the heat and, using a hand blender, blend until the soup is smooth. Alternatively, allow to cool a little before pouring into a blender or food processor. Pass the soup through a fine strainer into a clean saucepan.

This soup can be served hot or cold. If you want to serve hot, reheat gently. If you want it cold, set aside to cool, then refrigerate until you're ready to serve.

Potatoes Dauphinoise

Creamy, decadent, and irresistable, this classic potato dish is deceptively simple to make.

Preheat the oven to 325°F.

Place the cream, milk, thyme, peppercorns, and garlic in a large, heavy-bottomed saucepan and bring to a boil. Then remove the pan from the heat and set aside to allow the flavors to infuse.

Season the buttered baking dish with salt and pepper. Arrange the sliced potatoes in the dish, overlapping them until you have used them all up, and season each layer.

Pass the cream mixture through a fine strainer into a clean measuring cup or bowl, then pour it over the potatoes, ensuring that all of them are covered.

Bake in the oven for 45–55 minutes, until the potatoes are cooked and have absorbed the cream. Test by prodding them with a sharp knife. The potatoes should be soft and golden brown on top. If they look a little pale, place the dish under the broiler to give them color.

BRYN'S TIPS
For a twist on the dish, add some rutabaga or celery root to the potatoes. Just make sure that at least 60 percent of the dish is potato; it needs the potato starch in order to come together.

Serves 4–6

1⅔ cups heavy cream

⅓ cup milk

sprig of thyme

4 black peppercorns

2 garlic cloves, peeled and crushed

salt and pepper

1¼lb Desirée or Russet potatoes, peeled and thinly sliced

You will need a well-buttered 8in baking dish, about 1½in deep.

Potato Blinis

These little potato pancakes are wonderful served warm with some good smoked salmon and a dollop of sour cream or crème fraîche. I like to serve them with my Sunday brunch.

Place the flour, nutmeg, and salt in a large bowl. In a separate bowl, mix together the milk, whole egg, and the egg yolk, then pour the mixture onto the flour. Whisk everything together, then gently fold in the mashed potato. Set aside, uncovered, to cool.

When the mixture is cool, cover the bowl and leave it to rest in the refrigerator for up to 3 hours. The mixture should have a dropping consistency, so if it becomes too firm in the fridge, leave it at room temperature until it loosens up.

Heat the butter in a nonstick frying pan. Drop in a tablespoonful of the blini mixture and fry for 1–2 minutes on each side, until golden brown. Transfer to paper towels to drain. Repeat until all the mixture is used up, and serve hot.

BRYN'S TIPS
When I specify mashed potato in the ingredients list, I mean just mashed potato—no butter, no cream, no nothing.

Makes about 12

¾ cup all-purpose flour

1 tsp grated nutmeg

pinch of salt

⅓ cup milk

1 egg, plus 1 egg yolk

2 medium Desirée or Russet potatoes, peeled, boiled, and mashed (to give just over 4oz, or 1 cup, mashed potatoes)

¼ cup butter

Marjoram Gnocchi

Serves 4

3 large Desirée or Russet potatoes (to give just over 1lb mashed potatoes)

about ¾ cup rock salt

3 egg yolks

1⅓ cups "oo" flour (see tip, below)

½ cup freshly grated Parmesan

1 tsp salt

handful of fresh marjoram, finely chopped

Don't be afraid of making gnocchi. Although they look impressive, they are relatively uncomplicated to make. You could serve them simply, with a little butter and Parmesan, or as I love to do, with a piece of pan-fried fish and some fresh peas blended into a sauce—that flavor combination is magic. I use marjoram here, but you could substitute any fresh green herb, or even some chopped olives.

Preheat the oven to 325°F.

Place the unpeeled potatoes in a roasting pan lined with rock salt and bake in the oven until soft, about 1½ hours. When they are ready, remove the potatoes from the oven, carefully cut them in half—don't burn yourself on the steam—then scoop the warm potato out of the skin. Place in a large bowl and mash until smooth.

Add the egg yolks, 1 cup of the flour, the Parmesan, salt, and the marjoram and mix well until the ingredients come together as a dough. It should feel silky and pliable—like putty.

Divide the mixture into four pieces. Using the remaining flour to dust your hands and the work surface, roll each piece into a long sausage shape, about ½in in diameter. Cut each sausage into 1in lengths and place them on a floured board or tray. They should look like rows of little pillows! Don't worry if they're not all uniform—that's part of the charm.

Bring a large pan of salted water to a rolling boil. Drop the gnocchi into the water—you can probably cook half of them at once. Once the gnocchi start to float to the surface, they are ready. Remove from the water with a slotted spoon and serve hot.

BRYN'S TIPS

Don't throw away the potato skins after scooping out the flesh; deep-fry them in oil until crisp and golden, sprinkle with sea salt, and eat as a snack. I often serve these for our staff breaks with cheese and some Spiced Tomato Chutney (see page 252).

"oo" flour is traditionally used for making pasta. It is a coarsely ground durum wheat flour that holds the shape of the pasta or gnocchi during cooking and doesn't disintegrate.

Almond Potatoes

Essentially posh potato croquettes, these are great with braises and roasts, although, frankly, they go well with anything! If you don't like almonds, feel free to substitute bread crumbs.

Makes 12–16

1lb Desirée or Russet potatoes, peeled, boiled, and mashed

2 egg yolks

¼ cup butter, melted

salt and pepper

pinch of freshly grated nutmeg

¾ cup all-purpose flour

2 eggs, lightly beaten

1 cup flaked or chopped almonds

oil, for frying

Put the mashed potato in a large bowl. Add the egg yolks and the melted butter and mix well with a wooden spoon. Season to taste with salt, pepper, and fresh nutmeg.

Using your hands (you may want to flour them first), form the mixture into cylinder shapes, each one about 5 × 1in. Roll the cylinders gently in the flour, then in the beaten egg, and finish by rolling in the almonds until coated all over.

Place the cylinders in the refrigerator for 30 minutes to firm up, then fry them in a deep-fat fryer at 356°F for 1–2 minutes, until golden and crispy on the outside. If you don't have a deep-fat fryer, heat 2 tablespoons oil in a heavy-bottomed frying pan and gently shallow-fry the cylinders until golden brown. Drain briefly on paper towels before serving.

BRYN'S TIPS
As with other recipes in this chapter, the mashed potato should be purely mashed potato—don't add butter, cream, or any other ingredient.

Crab

We never really ate crab when I was growing up. Not even the canned variety. So it was a revelation when I finally got to taste and cook with this wonderfully versatile creature. I was—and still am—blown away by brown crab meat and am consistently amazed that people tend to eat only the white meat. The brown meat has such a depth of flavor and the texture is so rich and creamy, almost egglike.

I found, over the years, that many restaurants featured only dressed crab on the menu. And there's nothing wrong with that; it's a simple and delicious way of preparing and eating crab. But I wanted to mix things up a bit—to combine the dark and the light meats, and even make a feature of the dark meat.

Although there seems to be plenty of crab in our oceans, there is still some debate about how it is harvested and its sustainability. We are getting better at managing fisheries for crustaceans, but still have a ways to go. So it's important to ask questions when buying crab. Try to find out where it comes from and to source local crab, where possible. If you don't ask, you don't get, and our demand as customers drives supply.

Ask at the fish counter about different types of crab, too. I love to use spider crab when I can: the meat is so sweet and dense. With regard to the seasonality of crab, the tradition is that we should eat crab in the spring and summer months, but I have a supplier in South Wales who swears the meat is sweeter in the winter. But we always tend to have crab on the menu at the restaurant in the summer months, I have to say. The customers seem to expect it. And we always use the male crab. I think the females should be left in the sea to lay their eggs.

There is no waste on a crab either. Once you have enjoyed the sweet meat in any number of ways, don't throw away the shells. Break them up, put them in a roasting pan with some chopped onions, carrots, and celery, and roast in the oven at 225°F for about 20 minutes. Remove from the oven and *either* cover the shells and vegetables with some good olive oil, steep for 40 minutes or so, and then strain to make crab oil— this is fantastic drizzled on crab dishes—*or* just cover the roasted shells and vegetables with water and simmer over low heat for about 20 minutes to make a wonderful, rich, crabby stock to use in soups and risottos.

Crab Salad

Serves 4 as an appetizer

10oz white crab meat

juice of 1 lime

1 tbsp peanut oil

3–4 drops of Tabasco sauce

salt and pepper

1 scallion, trimmed and thinly sliced

2 tomatoes, peeled, chopped, and deseeded

4 basil leaves, torn

2 Little Gem lettuces, divided into leaves

In the summer months, this is always on the menu at the restaurant. It's fresh and light, with a hint of spice and spiked with lime and basil. It can either be an appetizer or a simple main course. Either way, I think it really showcases crab's clean, briny flavors.

Carefully pick any shell out of the white crab meat and place the meat in a bowl. Season with the lime juice, peanut oil, Tabasco sauce, salt, and pepper and mix everything together well.

Gently fold in the scallion, the tomatoes, and the basil, trying to keep the tomatoes intact.

Spoon the crab mixture into the lettuce leaves and serve cold.

Crab Risotto

A little unusual, but this combination really works—the rich, dark meat and the bright, light meat play against the creaminess of the risotto.

Pour the stock into a saucepan and bring to a boil over medium heat. Reduce to a simmer and keep the pan within easy reach until needed.

Now, heat the butter and the olive oil in a heavy-bottomed saucepan. Add the chopped shallots and cook for 2–3 minutes, or until soft. Add the rice, stir well to coat it with the butter and shallot mixture, then cook for another minute. Add the white wine, stirring continuously until all the liquid has been absorbed.

Add a ladleful of the simmering stock to the rice, stirring all the time, and cook until the stock has been absorbed before adding another ladleful. Repeat until the rice is tender but retains a little bite—this should take about 20 minutes. When the risotto is ready, season with salt and pepper. Then remove from the heat, put on a lid, and set aside to keep warm and rest a little.

Stir the Parmesan and the brown crab meat into the risotto. Add the white meat and the lemon juice, stirring gently. If the risotto feels a little firm, stir in some stock before serving. Serve with the lemon zest and parsley scattered over the top.

Serves 4–6 as an appetizer

1 quart Vegetable Stock (see page 257)

¼ cup butter

1 tbsp olive oil

2 shallots, peeled and finely chopped

1 cup risotto rice

⅓ cup white wine

salt and pepper

½ cup freshly grated Parmesan

4oz brown crab meat

2oz white crab meat

juice and zest of 1 lemon

2 tbsp chopped parsley

Crab on Toast

Serves 4–6

4oz white crab meat

2oz brown crab meat

2 egg yolks

1 tbsp bread crumbs

zest of 1 lemon

4 drops of Tabasco sauce

salt and pepper

6 slices of bread

This is a variation on Welsh Rarebit, and it makes a fantastic canapé or snack. It's so quick and simple that I often whip it up to eat after work in front of the TV. For a light supper, just serve it with a green salad.

Preheat the oven to 325°F.

Carefully pick any shell out of the white and brown crab meat and place the meat in a bowl. Add the egg yolks, bread crumbs, lemon zest, Tabasco sauce, and salt and pepper, and mix well. Set aside.

Lightly toast the bread on both sides. Spread the crab mixture evenly on each slice, then put on a baking sheet and place in the oven for 3–4 minutes, until the crab is hot. Serve immediately.

Crab Cocktail with Cucumber & Lime Jelly

This is my take on a traditional shrimp cocktail. Cucumber goes excellently with crab, so the jelly is a playful extension of this terrific combination. Make the jelly the day before you plan to serve the cocktail to give it time to set.

If using leaf gelatin, soak the gelatin following the instructions on the package. With a juicer, juice the cucumbers and reserve the liquid in a bowl.

Place half the cucumber juice in a saucepan and bring to a boil. Remove from the heat at once and add the strained, softened gelatin. Whisk well until the gelatin dissolves, then pass the liquid through a fine strainer onto the remaining juice. Add the lime juice and season with salt, to taste. Now divide the cucumber juice equally between 4 glasses or ramekins and place them in the refrigerator overnight to set.

In another bowl, mix the mayonnaise, ketchup, and the Worcestershire sauce together well to make the cocktail sauce.

To serve, top each of the set cucumber jellies with some of the shredded lettuce. Place a spoonful of the cocktail sauce on the lettuce, then cover with a quarter of the crab meat. Finish with another spoonful of cocktail sauce, a squeeze of lemon juice, and a scattering of the chopped egg.

BRYN'S TIPS
Spider crab is a terrific ingredient. Ask your fishmonger if he can source it for you, but if not, substitute any good white crab meat.

Serves 4

3 leaves gelatin (or half a ¼oz envelope of gelatin)

3 large cucumbers, cut in half and deseeded

juice of 1 lime

salt and pepper

9oz mayonnaise

2oz ketchup

1 tbsp Worcestershire sauce

½ iceberg lettuce, shredded

14oz white spider crab meat, cooked

1 lemon

2 hard-boiled eggs, chopped

Brown Crab Custard

Serves 4

5 eggs

7oz brown crab meat

⅔ cup heavy cream

⅓ cup milk

salt and pepper

pinch of grated nutmeg

toast strips, to serve

This resembles a savory crème brûlée—rich and smooth, but very crabby! That might sound unusual, but it's delicious, so I encourage you to try it out as an appetizer or a light supper dish.

Preheat the oven to 275°F.

In a large bowl, beat the eggs and set aside. Place the brown crab meat in a separate bowl, picking carefully through it to remove any shell, and set that aside, too.

Pour the cream and the milk into a heavy-bottomed saucepan and bring it to a boil. Immediately take the pan off the heat and pour the boiling cream over the beaten eggs. Stir well to combine. Then add the brown crab meat and stir in well. Season with salt, pepper, and nutmeg, and pour into individual ramekins.

Put the ramekins in a roasting pan, then pour warm water into the pan so that it reaches halfway up the side of the ramekins. This will help the custard to cook evenly. Bake in the oven for 25–30 minutes, then remove, and set aside to cool slightly. Serve warm with the toast strips.

Scallops

If you forced me to choose my number one favorite ingredient, scallops would win, hands down. That's why I always have a scallop dish on the menu at my restaurant. There's something about that milky flesh—so firm and sweet and fat—and its creamy, eggy coral. Eating scallops raw, straight from the shell, or perhaps with just a simple marinade, may just be one of life's better moments. The ocean flavor shines through.

My family taught me the importance of managing the land, and about our responsibility to the land. The same principles apply to the sea. At my restaurant, we use only diver-caught scallops, not just because they're more sustainable, but also because they taste better than dredged scallops. Diving ensures that only the adult scallops are harvested, and helps to manage their population. Dredging just fills the shells with grit and sand, while damaging the meat. So, please, do your best to find the best. I confess, though, that I've never dived for scallops myself. These mollosks thrive in cold water, and I prefer to dive where the sun has warmed things up a bit; basically, I'm too much of a chicken to brave the cold!

Some of you will think of scallops as a luxury ingredient and too expensive for everyday cooking. The truth is they do taste luxurious, and, as to the expense, just consider what you're paying for with diver-caught scallops. You are not just employing a man to spend time underwater hand-harvesting an adult shellfish just for you. You are also paying him to hand-manage the seafloor and to ensure the future of sustainable fishing. Not quite so expensive now, is it?

If I cannot get diver-caught scallops for the restaurant, I don't put them on the menu. That's that. But when I can, they arrive complete in the shell and we shuck and clean them ourselves, cutting them gently away from the shell and removing the frilly "skirt" that surrounds the meat and roe. We wash them quickly in lightly salted water and pat them dry with paper towels as soon as possible. You want them to go into the pan nice and dry, so they caramelize beautifully. As with any ingredient, the preparation is vitally important to the end product.

Scallops can live up to 20 years, but I am pretty sure they would be far too tough to chew at that age! The ones that are harvested for us are usually between 18 months and 2 years old. They're sweet and delicious, and singing with flavor. Actually, some folks hold that scallops really do sing. Fishermen of legend have sworn that they have heard their song. Science may tell us that's merely the whooshing sound they make as they propel themselves along, but I prefer the singing version of the story myself!

The important thing with scallops is to source them well—and the fresher, the better. They should be firm and plump, with a sweet, briny aroma, glossy coral, and creamy colored meat. Properly chosen, they offer some of the finest eating our seas can provide.

Raw Scallop Salad

This is natural beauty on a plate: raw, unadulterated scallops lightly dressed and served with tangy, aniseedlike fennel and peppery radishes. Totally fresh and light. Don't be scared of handling scallops, but if you prefer, you can have them shelled and cleaned at the fish counter.

Serves 4 as an appetizer

8 large scallops, roes removed (see tip, below)

sea salt and pepper

zest and juice of 1 lemon

2 tbsp olive oil

2 large fennel bulbs

8 radishes

a bunch of chives, finely chopped

Slice the scallops as thinly as possible and arrange them on a serving plate. Ensure that they do not overlap, because they need to marinate evenly.

Season the scallops with a pinch of salt, the lemon zest, and a little of the olive oil, and leave to marinate for 5 minutes.

Cut the fennel bulb in half and carefully remove the woody root. With a mandolin or very sharp knife, slice the fennel as thinly as possible. Place in a bowl, season with salt and pepper, the lemon juice, and the remaining olive oil.

Thinly slice the radishes lengthwise and add them to the fennel. Now add the chives and mix well. Scatter the fennel and radish mixture over the scallops and serve immediately. I like to serve the scallops on one platter as a centerpiece.

BRYN'S TIPS
If the corals (roes) are still attached to the scallops, just before serving the dish, quickly sear them on each side and use to top the dish.

Alternatively, bake the roes on a tray in the oven heated to its lowest setting (225°F) for about 2 hours, until very dry. Then process the roes to a powder in a food processor and store in a jar. I sprinkle this powder over risottos and pastas, and even on cheese straws just before baking.

Baked Scallops in the Shell

Serves 4 as an appetizer

2 tbsp butter

1 carrot, peeled and cut into thin strips

1 leek, trimmed and cut into thin strips

1–2 tbsp soy sauce

1 tbsp sesame oil

1oz stem ginger (from a jar), cut into thin strips

8 scallops, roes removed

salt and pepper

flour, for dusting

4oz puff pastry (ready-made is fine)

1 egg, beaten

about ¾ cup rock salt

You will need 4 scallop shells, top and bottom.

Asian flavors go so well with seafood. In this dish, the root vegetables give the scallop meat a platform on which to sit, so it never comes in contact with direct heat and stays deliciously moist. This is a great dinner-party appetizer, because it can be prepared up to four hours in advance. Keep it in the fridge until you are ready to bake it.

Preheat the oven to 350°F.

Melt the butter in a large, heavy-bottomed saucepan. Add the carrot and leek, and gently sweat them until they are soft. Take off the heat and set aside to cool.

When they are cool, place the vegetables in a large bowl. Add the soy sauce, sesame oil, and stem ginger, and mix well to combine. Set aside.

Cut each scallop in half. Divide the vegetable mixture evenly between the four larger scallop shells, then arrange four slices of scallop on top of each pile of vegetables. Season with salt and pepper to taste. Pour any remaining juices from the vegetable bowl over the top, then place the thinner shells on top to re-form whole scallops.

On a floured surface, roll out the puff pastry into an oblong shape, about 4 × 16in. Cut it into four even strips, then place one pastry strip around each scallop shell to seal the edges. Using your fingers, gently press the pastry into place to ensure that the seal is tight and there are no holes. Brush the pastry with the beaten egg.

Spread a bed of rock salt across a baking sheet, place each scallop shell on top—to stop them from wobbling—and cook in the oven for 10 minutes. To serve, carefully remove the top shell and eat the scallops from the bottom shell.

BRYN'S TIPS

Ask for scallop shells at the fish counter. Clean them thoroughly before using them in this dish, then reserve them for future dishes.

If you can't get scallop shells, cut four squares of foil and divide the vegetable mixture between them. Place the scallops on top. Fold over the foil to make a parcel, and crimp the edges to seal. Don't make the parcels too tight: the scallop meat needs space to cook evenly. Put the parcels on a baking sheet, scallop-side up, and bake as above. You will not need the layer of salt or the pastry.

Curried Scallops with Cauliflower & Coconut Soup

Serves 4 as an appetizer

¼ cup butter

1 small cauliflower, stalk removed and very finely chopped

1 cup Chicken Stock (see page 259)

½ cup coconut cream

pinch of salt

pinch of sugar

4 large scallops, roes removed

2 tsp curry powder

2 tbsp olive oil

1 lemon

I came up with this dish one winter, using the cauliflower for its earthy flavor, and the curry powder and coconut for richness and depth. This makes quite a thick, luxurious soup—if it were thinner, the scallops would sink.

Melt the butter in a large, heavy-bottomed saucepan without allowing it to color. Add the cauliflower and let it sweat gently for 2–3 minutes without coloring. Pour in the chicken stock, bring to a boil, and cook until the cauliflower is soft. Add the coconut cream and bring the pan back to a boil. Remove from the heat immediately—to preserve the cauliflower flavor—and, using a blender or food processor, blend until smooth. It will be hot, so be careful.

Pass the soup through a fine strainer into a clean saucepan, season with the salt and sugar, set aside, and keep warm.

Sprinkle the scallops evenly with the curry powder. Place a heavy-bottomed frying pan over medium heat until hot. Pour in the olive oil. Once it is hot, add the scallops and cook for 2 minutes on one side, then turn them over and cook for 30 seconds on the other side. Remove from the frying pan and season with salt and a squeeze of lemon juice.

To serve, pour the soup carefully into four shallow bowls and rest the scallops gently on top.

BRYN'S TIPS
By cooking the scallops for just 30 seconds on the second side, you ensure that they remain slightly undercooked in the center. Then the taste and texture are at their best—there's nothing worse than an overcooked, rubbery scallop. Let's treat this beautiful ingredient with the respect it deserves!

I prefer to use a medium-hot curry powder, but if you like it spicier, feel free to use a hot one.

Roast Scallops, Pork Belly, & Apricot

The fresh, briny scallop, the rich, fatty pork belly, and the sweet apricot and vanilla work together so well. This dish takes time, so I recommend that you cook and refrigerate the pork belly a day in advance.

Preheat the oven to 275°F. Rub the pork belly all over with 1 tablespoon of the olive oil, season generously with salt and pepper, and set aside.

Place the carrot, onion, and thyme in a suitably sized roasting pan, then place the pork belly on top of the vegetables, and put in the oven for 5–6 hours.

Remove the pork belly from the roasting pan. Pour the cooking juices into a clean saucepan and set aside. Place the meat on a clean baking sheet, then position another tray on top and add some weight to the top to ensure the pork belly keeps its shape— I use cans of beans. Let the belly cool to room temperature, then cover and place in the refrigerator until completely cold.

Once it is cold, remove the skin from the pork belly by gently peeling it off—you may need a paring knife to cut it away from the flesh—and discard. Cut the meat into 1in-thick slices and set aside.

In a heavy-bottomed saucepan, cover the apricots with cold water, add the vanilla pod and seeds, and bring to a boil. Simmer for 10–15 minutes, or until the apricots are soft. Remove and discard the vanilla pod. Place the apricots in a blender or food processor, add just enough of the cooking water to create a purée, and process. Pass the mixture through a fine strainer into a clean bowl and season to taste. Set aside and keep warm.

Now, gently heat the set-aside roasting juices from the pork, skimming off some of the excess fat—you need the flavor but not too much greasiness. Set aside and keep warm.

Heat a heavy-bottomed frying pan until very hot. Add the remaining olive oil. When it is hot, add the slices of pork belly and fry on both sides until crisp and golden brown, 2–3 minutes each. Remove with a slotted spoon, set aside, and keep warm.

Place the scallops in the hot pan and cook for 1 minute on one side, then turn them over and cook for 30 seconds on the other side. Remove from the frying pan and season with salt and a squeeze of fresh lemon juice. To serve, divide the scallops and crispy pork belly evenly between four plates. Spoon the apricot purée to the side and top with the cooking juices.

Serves 4 as an appetizer

9oz pork belly

2 tbsp olive oil

salt and pepper

1 carrot, peeled and cut in half

1 small onion, peeled and cut in half

sprig of thyme

4oz dried apricots

½ vanilla pod, split in half and seeds scraped out

8 scallops, roes removed

1 lemon

Seared Scallops, Braised Chicken Wings, & Jerusalem Artichokes

I love the creaminess of the Jerusalem artichokes against the squeaky scallops and crispy chicken wings. Because of the separate techniques involved, I recommend that you prepare the chicken wings the day before serving the dish.

First, joint the chicken wings: with a sharp knife, remove the tip and the third section, if there is one, from the wing and set aside. You need the middle portion of the wing only. Season with salt and pepper.

Place a heavy-bottomed frying pan over medium heat. When it is hot, melt ¼ cup of the butter, then place the chicken wings in the pan, skin-side down. Cook until golden brown all over, 2–3 minutes each. Remove from the pan and set aside.

Add the carrot and onion to the pan and cook until softened. Add the thyme and white wine. Bring to a boil, reduce to a simmer, and allow to reduce by half. Return the chicken wings to the pan, cover with 1⅔ cups of the stock, bring back to a boil, then reduce to a simmer for 30 minutes. Remove the pan from the heat and allow to cool.

When they are cold, take the wings out of the pan and remove the wing bones—just twist and pull. Discard the bones and place the meat on a plate in the fridge, to firm up.

Pass the stock and wine mixture through a fine strainer into a clean pan. Bring to a boil over medium heat and allow the sauce to reduce by half, until you have a light gravy. Set aside and keep warm.

To cook the artichokes, melt the remaining butter in a heavy-bottomed saucepan. Add the artichokes and season. Cover with the remaining chicken stock and cook until the artichokes are soft and all the stock has evaporated. Add the cream and transfer to a blender or food processor. Blend until smooth, adjust the seasoning, and set aside.

Place a frying pan over high heat until very hot. Add the olive oil, and when that's hot, add the scallops. Cook for 1 minute on one side, then turn over and cook for 30 seconds on the other side. Remove from the frying pan, season with fresh lemon juice, salt, and pepper, and set aside. Add the chicken wings to the same pan and crisp them up—about 1 minute on each side.

To serve, place two scoops of the Jerusalem artichoke purée into four large bowls, and place two scallops and two wings on top of each one. Finish the sauce by adding the hazelnuts, then pour it over the top.

Serves 4

8 chicken wings

salt and pepper

½ cup butter

1 medium carrot, peeled and chopped

1 medium onion, peeled and chopped

1 tbsp fresh thyme leaves

⅓ cup white wine

2 cups Chicken Stock (see page 259)

10oz Jerusalem artichokes, peeled and chopped

½ cup heavy cream

1 tbsp olive oil

8 large scallops, roes removed

1 lemon

½ cup chopped hazelnuts

Salmon

Salmon played a big part in my childhood, especially on the days when it was pouring with rain! My friends and I would jump on our bikes and ride off to the Ystrad River nearby— the site of our infamous apple fights (of which, more later).

There were salmon troughs in that part of the river—about four or five old stone structures over a 65-foot stretch of water. We'd spend hours watching the salmon leap high into the air as they bore themselves upstream to spawn. It is an extraordinary feat; the salmon fights its way back from the ocean, sometimes from as far as 1,000 miles away—where it has been for between one and seven years—back to the stream where it was born, to spawn its eggs in a safe environment. And then, just days later, it dies.

It was an extraordinary sight, and one we never tired of... that and splashing around, and trying to catch them.

Salmon is a magnificent fish, and—very important—its stocks can be managed both sustainably and sensibly to combat overfishing, and to maintain future fish stocks. Do try to buy wild salmon when in season in early summer: its flavor is truly wonderful. But when you can't get it, a responsibly farmed salmon is certainly an acceptable substitute. And don't forget, salmon is full of essential Omega 3 fatty acids that are incredibly good for you. It's not just another piece of fish.

Salmon is a classic nose-to-tail fish, too. There's not much of it you can't use. The skin is crispy and unctuous when fried, the roes are sweet and salty—just try them on the blinis on page 45 with a little crème fraîche. You can also roast the bones and add them to a stock pot for extra richness.

And, beyond its great flavor, salmon can stand up to all manner of cooking and curing. You can eat it raw, steamed, poached, roasted, or smoked. It holds its shape and takes on other flavors really well. When you are buying fresh salmon, look for bright, clear eyes and red gills. Its flesh should be a lovely pale orange-pink color. With smoked salmon, you want to look for a good pale-pink color and no oil floating on top. All the oil should be contained within the flesh to ensure moist, delicious fish.

Please, as ever, buy the best salmon you can afford. Try to find a fishmonger you really like and trust. He'll be able to guide you to a good-quality fish from a well-managed farm. And he'll be able to find you a delicious wild salmon, too, helping you appreciate and enjoy salmon all the more.

Potted Salmon, Horseradish, & Pickled Cucumber

Serves 4–6

For the pickled cucumber

4 cucumbers

1²⁄₃ cups white wine vinegar

1¼ cups superfine sugar

2 tbsp sea salt

1 garlic clove, peeled and crushed

1 red chile, split

sprig of thyme

1 bay leaf

For the potted salmon

1¼lb salmon fillet, skinless and boneless

salt and pepper

1 quart Vegetable Stock (see page 257)

juice and zest of 1 lemon

½ tbsp chopped chives

½ tbsp chopped chervil

3 tbsp horseradish sauce

1 cup unsalted butter, melted and slightly cooled

You will need sterilized preserving jars with lids (see page 245).

This makes a lovely appetizer. The horseradish cuts the richness of the salmon and the pickled cucumber lifts everything. It looks great, too. If you're pressed for time, you can eat the cucumbers right after making them, but they are best after a few days.

First, prepare the pickled cucumbers. Peel them and cut in half lengthwise. To remove the seeds, take a teaspoon and make a trench down the center, carefully scooping out the seeds. Cut the cucumber halves into 1in lengths, then slice each one into four sticks. Place in a bowl or pan and set aside.

Boil the vinegar, sugar, salt, garlic, and chile in a heavy-bottomed saucepan for 2 minutes, then add the thyme and bay leaf. Remove from the heat and pour the mixture over the cucumber. Cover with a lid or foil and set aside to cool. When they are completely cold, pour the cucumber and pickling juices into a sterilized preserving jar and seal tightly. Label with the date. The pickled cucumbers will keep for up to 3 months in the refrigerator.

Now, for the potted salmon. Season the salmon with salt and pepper, to taste. Bring the vegetable stock to a boil in a large, heavy-bottomed saucepan. Remove from the heat and add the salmon to the pan. Leaving the salmon in the stock, set it aside to cool.

Once the salmon has reached room temperature, remove it from the stock, flake it into large pieces, and place them in a clean bowl. Add the lemon juice and zest, the chives, chervil, horseradish sauce, and salt and pepper. Pour in ¾ cup of the melted butter and carefully fold everything together.

Divide the mixture evenly into individual ramekins. Pat the mixture down into the ramekins with the back of a spoon until the surface is flat. Pour the remaining melted butter evenly over the top, making sure you cover the salmon with at least ¼in of butter. Then place the ramekins in the refrigerator to chill.

Take the potted salmon out of the refrigerator 30 minutes before serving. Serve with toast, salad leaves, and some pickled cucumber.

BRYN'S TIPS
See the note on pin bones and pin-boning on page 81, and find out how to make your own horseradish sauce on page 92.

Marinated Salmon, Avocado, & Wasabi Purée

Fresh, simple, and elegant, this is my play on sushi. It makes a great summer lunch, or an appetizer before a more robust main course. The salt, sugar, and spices lightly "cure" the salmon so that it is not completely raw. Note that this process takes some time, so it's best to start the recipe the day before you plan to serve it.

First, cure the salmon. In a bowl, mix together the salt, sugar, orange zest, lemon zest, lime zest, and black pepper. Place the salmon in a shallow dish and rub the marinade in well on both sides of the fish. Cover the salmon with plastic wrap and place in the refrigerator for 8 hours.

Once the time is up, wash the salmon as quickly and as thoroughly as possible, rinsing off all the marinade so that it doesn't continue to cure the fish. Set the salmon aside on paper towels to dry.

Now, make the sauces. Put the avocados in a blender or food processor with the lime juice, lemon juice, and wasabi, and blend until smooth—aim for the texture of thick yogurt. If the mixture seems rather dense, add a little cold water, but be careful not to add too much. Season with salt and pepper, to taste.

In a separate bowl, whisk together the soy sauce and the honey until well combined.

To serve, spread some avocado mix on individual plates. Arrange the salmon on top, scatter with pickled ginger and cress, and drizzle with the soy-honey dressing.

BRYN'S TIPS

I use a spiced salt from Halen Môn in North Wales, which is a Welsh organic sea salt. But don't worry if you can't find spiced salt—just use a good sea salt instead.

Pin bones are tiny bones that are not fused to the salmon's main skeleton. This means that they remain in the fish flesh after filleting. You can ask to have them removed at the fish counter, or you can easily do it yourself. Feel your way along the side of the salmon with your fingers. When you find a sharp little bone, grab it with a clean pair of tweezers or pliers and pull it out. Depending on the size of the fish, there should be about 12 on each side.

Serves 4–6

For the salmon

3 tsp spiced sea salt (see tip, below)

3 tsp sugar

zest of 1 orange

zest of 1 lemon

zest of 1 lime

pinch of black pepper

1¼lb salmon fillet, skinned, pin-boned (see tip, below), and cut into bite-sized pieces

For the sauces

2 avocados, peeled, pitted, and diced

juice of 1 lime

juice of ½ lemon

1 tsp wasabi paste

salt and pepper

3 tbsp soy sauce

1 tbsp honey

1 tbsp pickled ginger

handful of cress

Smoked Salmon Risotto

1 quart Smoked Salmon Stock (see page 259)

¼ cup unsalted butter

1 tbsp olive oil

2 shallots, peeled and finely chopped

1 cup risotto rice

⅓ cup white wine

white pepper

juice and zest of 1 lemon

½ cup freshly grated Parmesan

4oz smoked salmon, cut into ribbons

1 tbsp finely chopped flat-leaf parsley

A sexy, sophisticated, and very pretty appetizer. You could add some cooked asparagus to turn the dish into a delicious light lunch.

Pour the stock into a saucepan and bring to a boil over medium heat. Reduce to a simmer and keep the pan within reach until needed.

Heat the butter with the olive oil in a heavy-bottomed saucepan. Add the chopped shallot and cook for 2–3 minutes, or until soft. Add the rice, stir well to coat it with the butter and shallot mixture, then cook for another minute. Pour in the white wine and stir continuously until all the liquid has been absorbed.

Add a ladleful of the simmering stock to the rice and, stirring all the time, cook until the stock has been absorbed before adding another ladleful. Repeat until the rice is tender but retains a little bite—this should take about 20 minutes. When the risotto is ready, season with pepper, remove from the heat, put a lid on, and set aside to rest for a few minutes.

Stir the lemon juice and the Parmesan into the risotto, then fold in the smoked salmon. Serve the risotto with a scattering of the parsley and lemon zest.

Salmon, Peas, & Bacon

This has to be one of my all-time favorite flavor combinations. The salty cured bacon cuts through the dense fattiness of the salmon, and the peas and lettuce lend a top note of sweet freshness.

Blanch the peas and the carrot sticks in a large saucepan of boiling water until just tender. Remove from the pan with a slotted spoon, setting the pan aside, and immediately refresh the vegetables by plunging them into a bowl of ice-cold water to stop them from cooking. Drain well and set aside. Return the saucepan of water to the heat, bring back to a boil, and blanch the bacon for 1 minute. Drain well.

Melt 1 tbsp of the butter in a wide saucepan over medium heat. When it starts to foam, add the bacon, and cook until brown. Add the carrots and peas and cover with the chicken stock. Bring to a boil and cook for 5 minutes. Season well with salt and pepper, then add the remaining butter a little at a time, shaking the pan so that it emulsifies and thickens the sauce. Set aside and keep warm.

Dry the salmon skin thoroughly. With a very sharp knife, cut diagonal slashes in the skin and season with salt and pepper.

Heat a heavy-bottomed frying pan. Once it is hot, add the olive oil. When that has heated up, too, add the fish, skin-side down, and cook for 4–5 minutes, until the skin is crispy. Turn off the heat, then turn the fish over in the pan to warm the underside.

Just before serving, gently fold the shredded lettuce and horseradish sauce into the pea and bacon mixture. To serve, pour the bacon, peas, and lettuce into a deep bowl and place the salmon on top.

Serves 4

1½ cups fresh or frozen peas (thawed, if frozen)

1 medium carrot, peeled and cut into small sticks

2oz smoked bacon, cut into thin strips

½ cup unsalted butter, cubed

⅔ cup Chicken Stock (see page 259)

salt and pepper

4 salmon fillet steaks, skin on, about 5oz each

1 tbsp olive oil

1 Little Gem lettuce, trimmed and shredded

1 tbsp horseradish sauce

BRYN'S TIPS
For perfectly crispy fish with moist flesh, first dry the skin thoroughly. Make diagonal slashes in it and season with salt and pepper. Have a hot pan ready, then pour in a little oil—it is important to heat the pan before adding the oil. Put in the fish, skin-side down, and leave for 4–5 minutes. Keep watching (this requires instinct) and don't move the fish before the time's up or it won't crisp, and you may tear the skin or break the flesh. Then place the fish in the oven—without playing with it—for a few minutes to finish off. When the fish is cooked, turn it onto a plate, skin-side up.

For instructions on making your own horseradish sauce, see page 92.

Pan-fried Salmon with Curried Mussels

Serves 4

4 pieces of salmon fillet, about 4½oz each

2 tbsp vegetable oil

For the mussels

2½lb mussels

1 tbsp olive oil

1 onion, peeled and chopped

handful of parsley, chopped

salt and pepper

¾ cup white wine

For the sauce

¼ cup butter

1 onion, peeled and diced

1 medium carrot, peeled and diced

1 celery stick, trimmed and diced

1 tsp medium curry powder

½ cup heavy cream

4oz potatoes, peeled and diced

1 tbsp chopped chives

1 lemon

I love salmon and I love curry. So I thought I'd take a lovely piece of fish and pair it with this variation on a classic French mouclade. I think it takes two sustainable and easy-to-find ingredients and brings them right up to date. There are quite a few steps in this recipe, so read it carefully before you begin.

Preheat the oven to 350°F. Scrub and debeard the mussels. Discard any that are open.

Heat the olive oil in a large, heavy-bottomed pan that has a lid. Add the onion and the parsley, and soften. Add the mussels, salt and pepper, and the white wine. Bring to a boil, put the lid on, and shake the mussels around. Then leave the pan on the heat and cook until all the mussels are open, 3–5 minutes. Discard any that remain closed.

Strain the mussels and set aside, reserving the cooking liquid. Pour the liquid through a fine strainer into a clean pitcher to remove any grit.

To make the sauce, melt the butter in a saucepan over low heat. Sweat the onion, carrot, and celery, until soft. Stir in the curry powder and cook gently for a few minutes. Add ½ cup of the cooking liquid from the mussels, stir in well, and cook for another minute.

Dry the salmon skin thoroughly. With a very sharp knife, cut diagonal slashes in the skin and season with salt and pepper.

Heat a nonstick frying pan over medium heat, then add the vegetable oil. Cook the salmon, skin-side down, until the skin is crisp, 4–5 minutes. Then place the fish in the oven for 3–4 minutes.

Stir the heavy cream into the curried vegetable mixture, bring back to a boil, add the diced potatoes, and cook until softened, about 5 minutes. Remove the mussels from their shells, add them to the cream mixture, and warm them through.

Finish the sauce with the chopped chives and season with salt and pepper and a squeeze of lemon juice. To serve, place the curried mussels in a large bowl and arrange the salmon fillets on top.

Sole

Whenever I tell people how good sole is, they almost always reply that it's expensive. So let's be clear about this: Dover sole is expensive; lemon sole (sometimes called winter flounder in North America) isn't. In fact, it's really good value for money. The flesh tastes amazing, and all those finny off-cuts are great for the stock pot.

People often opt for plaice when looking for a cheaper flat fish. And plaice is a perfectly good fish, don't get me wrong. It's just not as user-friendly as sole. Sole is more robust—you can do much more with it, thanks to its dense flesh and deep flavor, both of which make it a more versatile ingredient to work with. You can also cook it both on and off the bone.

When I was a kid, we didn't eat so much fish. In fact, if I'm honest, fish sticks were about as far as I got (which is why I've included my version of this childhood staple here, for fun). It wasn't until my teens that I started catching fish, eating it, and learning to love it. Now I cannot get enough.

But with fish it is often difficult to know which varieties we should be buying and which we should avoid. As with game, we *can* manage wild stocks successfully to rebuild sustainable fisheries—and it's up to all of us to do our part. My best advice is, if you're not sure what to buy, ask for advice at the fish counter. Remember to ask to have the sole skinned for you, too—both the top, which is covered in a brown skin, and the belly, which is deceptively white, so people often forget about it. I say this because sole cooks so quickly that the skin never has a chance to become crispy. Keep any off-cuts for the stock pot, or more substantial pieces to bread and make into tasty goujons (breaded and deep-fried strips of fish).

We use lemon sole at the restaurant, and the recipes in this chapter really showcase its versatility. The funny thing is— lemon sole is a bit of a misnomer: it's neither sole (it's actually a flounder) nor does it taste of lemons! But it is a moist, delicious, and very reasonably priced fish, so try some today.

Lemon Sole Fish Sticks

Fish sticks as you've never had them! These are easy to make and taste fantastic. Serve them with my homemade Ketchup (see page 262) and fries, or with the Avocado & Wasabi Purée on page 81.

Season the flour with salt and pepper. Then season the beaten eggs with salt and pepper. Gently pass the sole fillets through the flour, shaking off any excess, then dip them into the beaten egg, coating them well. Finish the fish sticks by rolling the sole in the bread crumbs.

Heat some oil in a deep-fat fryer to 356°F. Fry the fish sticks for 4–6 minutes, until golden all over. If you don't have a deep-fat fryer, gently shallow-fry the fish sticks in a little oil for about 10 minutes, turning them occasionally, until they are golden brown.

Remove the fish sticks from the oil, drain on paper towels, season with salt, and serve with a wedge of lemon.

Serves 4

2 cups all-purpose flour

salt and pepper

3 eggs, beaten

4 lemon sole, skinned, filleted, and cut in half lengthwise

2 cups Japanese Panko bread crumbs (see tip, below)

oil, for frying

lemon wedges, to serve

BRYN'S TIPS
Panko is a flaky variety of bread crumb with a light, crispy texture. If you can't find this ingredient, substitute regular bread crumbs.

Roast Sole, Peas, & Horseradish

Serves 4

4 lemon sole, trimmed and skinned

salt and pepper

3 tbsp olive oil

¼ cup butter

¾ cup Creamed Fish Sauce (see page 260)

1½ cups fresh or frozen peas, cooked

2 tbsp horseradish sauce

This is a superb flavor combination, and the addition of the Creamed Fish Sauce lends the dish a really luxurious taste. If you don't like fish bones on your plate, you can take the flesh off the bone after you've cooked it. The reason to cook the sole on the bone is that it gives more flavor and keeps it moist.

Season the sole with salt and pepper. Heat a large, heavy-bottomed frying pan over medium heat. Add the olive oil, and, once it is hot, put in the sole and cook for 3–4 minutes. Add the butter and let it melt and foam up, then turn over the sole and cook for another 3–4 minutes. Remove the fish and set aside.

Bring the fish sauce to a boil in a saucepan. Add the cooked peas, and season with salt and pepper. Stir in the horseradish sauce just before serving.

To serve, place the sole on individual plates and the sauce in a bowl on the side.

BRYN'S TIPS
To make a simple, white horseradish sauce, combine 1 cup sour cream, 3 tablespoons finely grated, peeled, fresh horseradish root (use the smallest holes on a box grater), and several grindings of freshly ground black pepper. Taste the sauce and add more horseradish, if desired. Fresh horseradish has an intense flavor and heat, which is why you should start with a small amount and only add more horseradish if you like your sauce with a kick.

Broiled Sole with Fennel Salad

Fish and fennel go so wonderfully together, and I love the simplicity of broiled sole, so this dish seems to me like a match made in heaven.

Using a mandolin or a very sharp knife, slice the fennel as thinly as possible. Place it in a bowl and season with salt and pepper, the lemon juice, and the olive oil. Leave to marinate for about 10 minutes.

Add the radishes to the fennel, mixing them together well, then finish the salad with the chopped chives.

Mix the butter, the lemon juice and zest, the thyme, and salt and pepper in another bowl. Using a pastry brush or your fingers, coat the sole with the butter. Set any remaining butter aside.

Put the sole on a baking sheet and place under a preheated broiler for 6–8 minutes, or until the flesh comes away from the bone. An alternative to broiling is to pan-fry the sole: heat a pan over medium heat and fry the fish for 3–4 minutes on each side, until cooked.

If you have any butter left over, brush the fish again before serving. To serve, place each sole on a plate with a pile of salad beside it.

Serves 4

For the salad

2 fennel bulbs, trimmed, cut in half and cored

salt and pepper

juice of 1 lemon

3 tbsp olive oil

6 radishes, sliced lengthwise

a bunch of chives, finely chopped

For the fish

½ cup butter, softened

juice and zest of 1 lemon

1 tsp fresh thyme leaves

4 lemon sole, trimmed and skinned

Sole in a Bag with Zucchini & Black Olives

Serves 4

1 scallion, trimmed and thinly sliced

1 yellow zucchini, trimmed and thinly sliced

1 green zucchini, trimmed and thinly sliced

2oz black olives, pitted and cut in half

a bunch of basil

salt and pepper

1 tbsp olive oil

3 lemon sole, skinned and filleted to make 12 fillets

¼ cup butter

3 tbsp white wine

I love the colors and flavors of this dish. The black olives and basil add a salty, herbal tang, but the overall effect is surprisingly delicate. I like to serve these parcels just as they are, so people can open them up at the table. The steam billows out and the aroma hits diners smack in the face. It's really theatrical, and so much fun.

Preheat the oven to 350°F.

Place the scallion, yellow zucchini, green zucchini, black olives, and basil in a bowl. Season with salt and pepper, pour the olive oil over the top, and mix together well.

Cut four pieces of parchment paper or foil, each one measuring about 12 × 12in. Divide the vegetables into four equal piles on the pieces of parchment paper or foil. Place three sole fillets on each of the vegetable mounds, and fold each fillet in half to prevent them from overcooking. Season the sole with salt and pepper. Divide the butter evenly between each pile. Then fold the paper or foil over to create four parcels and, before you close them, pour a quarter of the white wine into each one. Seal the parcels tightly by folding over the edges and crimping them together. Leave a little space inside the parcels for the steam.

Place a large, heavy-bottomed frying pan or roasting pan over high heat and place the parcels in it. When the parcels start to expand, remove them from the heat and place in the oven for 7 minutes. Remove and serve at once.

Steamed Sole with Butternut Squash Tortellini

This recipe was inspired by traditional Italian pumpkin ravioli. I started by thinking how well pumpkin would go with shrimp, then suddenly the whole thing came together. Homemade tortellini make a big difference to the overall flavor of the dish.

Preheat the oven to 325°F.

Season the fleshy side of the butternut squash halves. Wrap them in foil and bake in the oven for 1 hour, or until soft; check by piercing with a knife. When the squash is ready, scrape out the flesh with a spoon and place in a bowl. Season to taste, and leave to cool.

Next, make the pasta. In a large bowl, mix together the olive oil and the egg. Put the flour and a pinch of salt in a food processor and, with the motor running, slowly add the oil and egg mixture until the mixture resembles fine bread crumbs. Then, using your hands, bring it together to create a dough that is firm to the touch and fairly dry. Depending on the size of the eggs, you may need to add 1 tablespoon of water to help the dough come together. Place the pasta dough on a clean, lightly floured work surface and knead it for 3–5 minutes. Wrap the dough in plastic wrap and place it in the refrigerator to rest for at least 1 hour.

Set the pasta machine to its thickest setting and pass one piece of dough through the rollers. Change the setting to the next-thickest and pass the sheet through the machine again. Repeat, keeping each sheet as wide as the machine and reducing the thickness setting each time until you have rolled the sheet through the thinnest setting.

Now, cut eight 3in disks from the pasta—use a well-floured, straight-edged cookie cutter. Place a teaspoon of the butternut mixture onto each of the pasta circles. Dip your finger in water and run it around the edge of the disk. Fold it over to create a half circle and press down to seal it. Then bring the two ends together to create each tortellino.

Next, prepare the fish and sauce. Season the sole. Roll up each sole fillet, thick end first, thin end last, and secure each one with a toothpick. Set aside.

Set a steamer over medium heat. When the water is boiling, place the sole rolls in the steamer and cook for 6–8 minutes. Meanwhile, bring a large pan of salted water to a boil. Cook the tortellini for 3–4 minutes, then remove them from the water immediately.

Meanwhile, bring the fish sauce to a boil in a small saucepan. Add the cucumber, brown shrimp, and chives, and season with the lemon juice. Remove from the heat. To serve, divide the sole and the tortellini evenly between plates and spoon the sauce over the top.

Serves 4

1 butternut squash, cut in half

salt and pepper

3 lemon sole, skinned and filleted to make 12 fillets

For the pasta

1 tbsp olive oil

1 egg

1¼ cups "00" flour, plus extra for dusting (see tip on page 46)

For the sauce

1 cup Creamed Fish Sauce (see page 260)

1 small cucumber, deseeded and diced

2oz brown shrimp

1 tbsp chopped chives

juice of 1 lemon

You will need a steamer, a pasta machine, and 12 toothpicks.

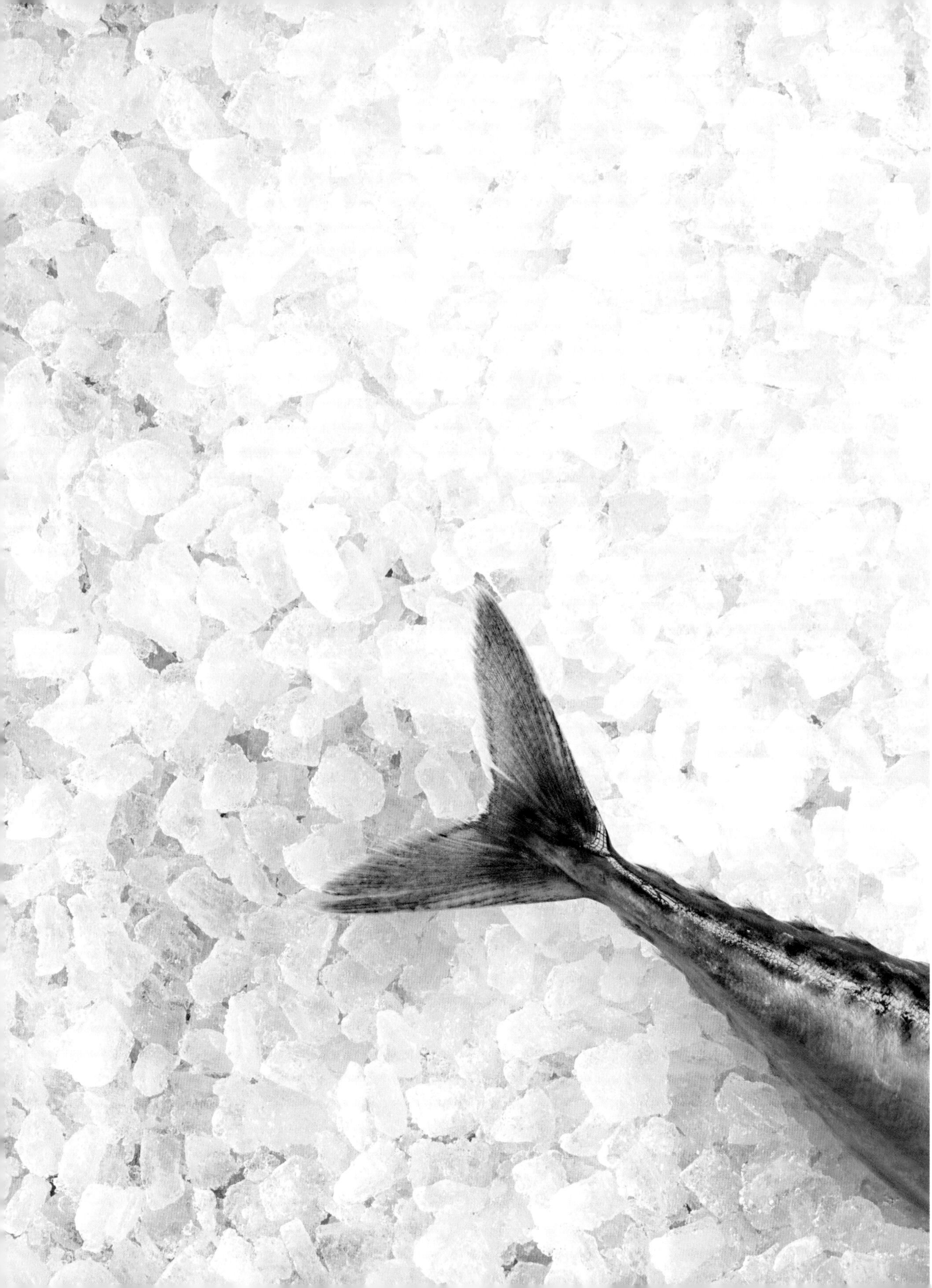

Mackerel

Mackerel

Glistening, blue-black, and packed with so many healthy fatty acids, mackerel is an amazing fish—so it's hard to believe that even as recently as 30 years ago it was pretty unpopular. It was thought of as a scavenger, and there were even wives' tales that mackerel lived on the bones of dead sailors. But at least that means there are still plenty of these fabulous fish in our seas. They are very cheap, full of flavor, and very, very good for you—full of Omega 3, vitamin B12, and selenium. So... they're healthy *and* delicious!

Mackerel might have been the first fish I ever caught. We went on a family vacation to the Isle of Anglesey, off the northwest coast of Wales, camping by the sea, and I managed to catch three on one line. Needless to say, I was hooked, too, and have been fishing ever since.

Mackerel is still easy to catch. Its stock numbers are one of the real success stories in marine stewardship, making this a good, responsible choice at the fish counter. Look for a fish that has a nice shiny body, bright clear eyes, and firm flesh. Unlike some fish that won't suffer too much from an extra day on the slab, mackerel should be bought when it's superfresh, to enjoy it at its best—especially if you plan to eat it raw or lightly marinated. Your fishmonger will be able to help you find a good one. He'll also prepare it just as you want it, but if you should choose to fillet it yourself, here's a quick tip to remove the pin bones with a V-cut. Slide your knife into the fillet, along each side of dorsal line, just down to but not through the skin. Now you can pull the pin bones (and some of the blood line), clean out of the fillet, and it's ready to cook.

A lot of people don't eat the skin on a fish, and with mackerel that's a real shame. There's so much flavor here. Make sure you get it nice and crispy. A whole mackerel on the barbecue is one of my absolute favorite summer treats, its skin crunchy and blistered from the heat.

Mackerel is a regular lunchtime favorite on the menu at my restaurant, Odette's. It's a fish that is capable of great versatility, its dense oiliness pairing well with bold flavors, as the recipes in this chapter demonstrate. Its current popularity is well-earned.

Salt & Vinegar Cured Mackerel

I ate something similar to this—a salt-and-vinegar cured bream—in Miami and thought how fantastic mackerel would be in the dish. This dish is delicious with the Beet Purée on page 20.

Place the sliced mackerel on a serving dish. Mix the vinegar and oil together in a bowl, and brush the mixture all over the mackerel. Season with a large pinch of the sea salt.

Dress the shallot rings and sliced radishes with the remaining dressing. Arrange them evenly over the mackerel.

Scatter the lemon zest and garden cress over the top. Season with freshly ground pepper, and serve immediately.

BRYN'S TIPS
Chardonnay vinegar is widely available, but if you can't get it, use the best white-wine vinegar you can find. Then the dressing won't taste too sharp.

Serves 4

6 large mackerel fillets, skinned and sliced as thinly as possible (like smoked salmon)

3 tbsp chardonnay vinegar (see tip, below)

$\frac{1}{3}$ cup olive oil

good, coarse sea salt and pepper

1 shallot, peeled and sliced into rings

2 radishes, trimmed and sliced

zest of 1 lemon

2oz garden cress

Grilled Mackerel, Fava Beans, & Chorizo

Serves 4 as an appetizer

olive oil, for greasing

salt and pepper

4 mackerel fillets, cut in half

2oz cooking chorizo, diced

1 shallot, peeled and very finely chopped

⅔ cup Chicken Stock (see page 259)

2½oz fava beans (thawed, if frozen)

1 tbsp finely chopped parsley

I love this combination. The spicy chorizo cuts against the oily fish, and the fava beans provide a lovely cushion to their big flavors.

Oil a baking sheet and season it generously with salt and pepper. Place the mackerel fillets on the baking sheet, flesh-side down, and place the baking sheet under the broiler until the fish are cooked—you should be able to see when they are done. Try to keep the mackerel flesh a little pink in the middle.

If you prefer, you can pan-fry the fish instead. Heat the pan over medium heat, then add 1 tablespoon olive oil. Once it is hot, add the mackerel fillets to the pan, skin-side down, and season the flesh with salt and pepper. Cook for 3–4 minutes, then turn them over for another minute, to finish.

Place the diced chorizo into a frying pan over medium heat. Cook for 4–5 minutes, or until the reddish oils have been released. Add the shallot and cook until soft. Pour the chicken stock over the top, bring to a boil, and simmer for another 3–4 minutes. Add the fava beans and bring back to a boil. Finally, add the chopped parsley and season to taste with salt and pepper. You should now have a thick broth.

To serve, pour the chorizo and fava beans, with some of their broth, into individual bowls and place the crisp mackerel fillets on top.

Mackerel Pâté

Serves 4

⅓ cup olive oil, plus extra for greasing

1 shallot, peeled and finely chopped

pinch of cayenne pepper

1 garlic clove, peeled and finely chopped

½ cup butter

salt and pepper

8 large mackerel fillets

juice and zest of 1 lemon

pinch of grated nutmeg

Enjoy this big, flavorful pâté as an appetizer or as part of a picnic. I like to serve it with the Pickled Cucumber on page 78 and some crisp toast.

Heat the olive oil in a heavy-bottomed saucepan. Add the shallot, cayenne pepper, and garlic and cook for 3–4 minutes, until the shallot is soft but not colored—be careful not to boil the oil. Remove the pan from the heat and set aside. In another saucepan, gently melt the butter, set it aside, and keep warm.

Oil a baking sheet and season it with salt and pepper. Place the mackerel fillets on the baking sheet, flesh-side down, and place the baking sheet under a hot broiler until the fish are cooked—you should be able to see when they are done. Try to keep the mackerel flesh a little pink in the middle. Set the baking sheet aside, to cool.

If you prefer, you can pan-fry the fish instead. Heat the pan over medium heat, then add 1 tablespoon olive oil. Once the oil is hot, add the mackerel fillets to the pan, skin-side down, and season the flesh with salt and pepper. Cook for 3–4 minutes, then turn them over for another minute, to finish.

When the mackerel has cooled, remove the skin, loosely break up the flesh, and put it in a blender or food processor. Pour in the shallot and oil mixture, then blend everything by pulsing a few times—make sure to keep some texture in the mackerel. Pour in the warm melted butter, the lemon juice and zest, and the nutmeg. Pulse the machine a few times again, scraping down the sides as you go to ensure that everything mixes thoroughly. Season with salt and pepper, to taste.

Divide the mixture between four ramekins, or put into one larger dish. Cover loosely and leave to cool. When cold, cover with plastic wrap and refrigerate for a couple of hours. Serve with warm toast, pickled cucumber, and some salad.

Bryn's Tips
If you would like to save the pâté for a few days, seal the top by pouring a little melted butter over the top once the pâté is cold.

Mackerel Salad

The flavors of this dish are so fresh and vibrant and yet it is a great pantry favorite, since the only fresh ingredients you need are mackerel, shallots, and parsley.

In a large bowl, mix together the pasta, shallots, black olives, capers, piquillo peppers, and parsley. Season the salad with salt and pepper, add the olive oil and balsamic, and set aside.

Oil a baking sheet and season it well with salt and pepper. Place the mackerel fillets on the baking sheet, flesh-side down, and place the sheet under a hot broiler until the fish is cooked—you should be able to see when it is done. Try to keep the mackerel flesh a little pink in the middle.

If you prefer, you can pan-fry the fish instead. Heat the pan over medium heat, then add 1 tablespoon olive oil. When it is hot, add the mackerel fillets to the pan, skin-side down, and season the flesh with salt and pepper. Cook for 3–4 minutes, then turn over for another minute to finish.

To serve, place each warm mackerel fillet on a plate with some of the salad on the side, and drizzle a little olive oil and balsamic vinegar over the top.

BRYN'S TIPS
Piquillo peppers—small red peppers roasted over embers—are available in jars and are a fantastic ingredient to keep in your pantry.

Serves 4 as an appetizer or light lunch

2oz orzo pasta, cooked

2 shallots, peeled and thinly sliced

3½oz black olives, pitted and cut in half

1oz capers, drained

2½oz piquillo peppers, quartered (see tip, below)

a bunch of flat-leaf parsley, finely chopped

salt and pepper

3 tbsp olive oil, plus extra for greasing and drizzling

2 tbsp balsamic vinegar, plus extra for drizzling

4 large mackerel fillets

Marinated Mackerel

*Serves 4 as an appetizer
or light main course*

1 cup olive oil, plus extra
for greasing

salt and pepper

4 large mackerel fillets

1 onion, peeled and sliced

1 carrot, peeled and sliced

1 garlic clove, peeled
and sliced

1 tsp coriander seeds

pinch of saffron

½ cup white wine

⅓ cup white wine vinegar

juice and zest of 1 lemon

1 tbsp finely chopped parsley

In this dish, the fish is both cured and cooked, giving it some terrific textures and flavors. Mackerel is resilient and robust enough to take this treatment. The coriander and saffron add an exotic dimension.

Oil a deep baking pan and season it well with salt and pepper. Place the mackerel fillets in the pan, flesh-side down, and place the pan under a hot broiler until the fish are cooked—you should be able to see when they are done. Try to keep the mackerel flesh a little pink in the middle. Set aside in the baking pan and keep warm.

If you prefer not to broil the fish, you can pan-fry it instead. Heat the pan over medium heat, then add 1 tablespoon olive oil. When it is hot, add the mackerel fillets to the pan, skin-side down, and season the flesh with salt and pepper. Cook for 3–4 minutes, then turn over for another minute, to finish. Transfer the fish to a warm, deep baking pan, skin-side up, and set aside.

Pour ⅓ cup of the olive oil into a large saucepan and heat it over medium heat. Add the onion, carrot, garlic, coriander seeds, and saffron, and cook for 3–4 minutes, without allowing them to color. Pour in the white wine and the vinegar and let it bubble until reduced by half.

When the liquid is reduced and the vegetables are soft, remove the saucepan from the heat. Pour in the remaining olive oil and the juice and zest of the lemon. Stir to combine.

Pour the mixture around the warm mackerel (avoiding the crispy skin), and leave to cool to room temperature. Once it is cool, transfer to a serving platter. Finish with the chopped parsley and serve with some salad and bread and butter.

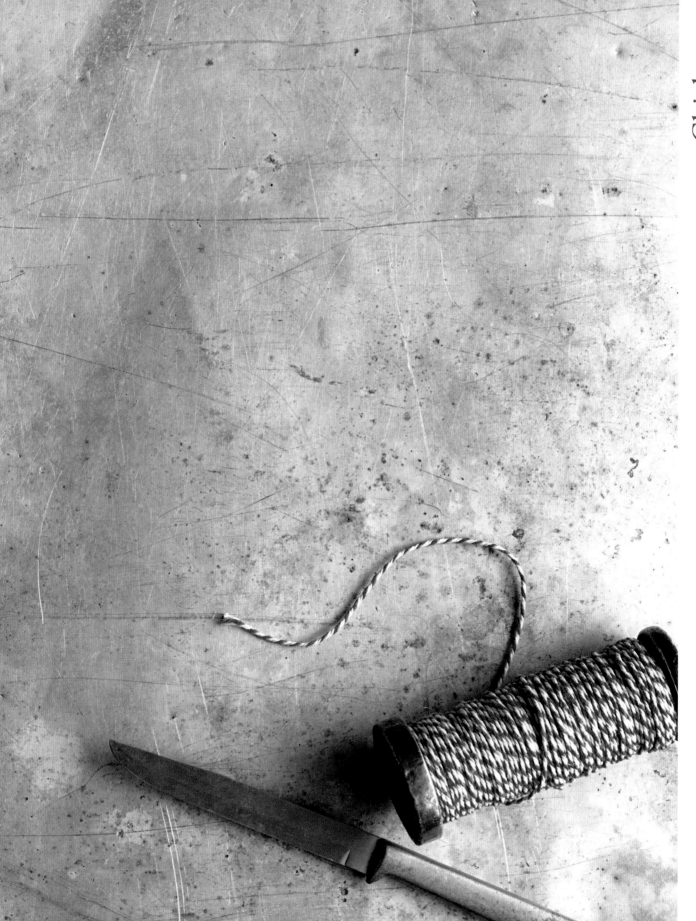

Chicken

Everyone loves chicken. If you took a quick poll of favorite home-cooked meals, odds are that the favorite would be roast chicken. At the same time, lots of people say that chicken is boring. But you can make anything exciting—especially chicken. It's how you source it and cook it that makes the difference. I always use free-range chickens from the Rhug Estate in Corwen, North Wales. A chicken that has had the chance to run around and scratch in the dirt will always, always taste better than one that's been caged. So try to use the best-quality birds you can find.

The chicken is a great friend to the farmer. It is the ultimate sustainable farmyard animal, giving eggs and manure as well as its own meat. We always had rusty-colored chickens running around the farm, mostly for eggs, but I'm sure the occasional bird made it to the pot or into a chicken pot-pie.

The chicken is such a versatile culinary creature, too. Aside from the obvious cuts, there are the livers, which can be sautéed, pan-fried, and made into pâtés and mousses (see page 120), tossed into salads or piled onto buttered toast for supper. Not enough people use chicken livers, which are cheap, plentiful, and delicious. Chicken flesh itself is very forgiving, and each cut has a different strength. The breasts are always fine for roasting or poaching; the legs are good for braising and long-cooking in sauces, the thighs, too—they don't fall apart and they keep their shape nicely. The wings are great on the barbecue, since the meat sticks to the bone and the pieces stay firm enough to pick up and eat. All the trimmings can go into the stock pot. Even the skin can be dried off and fried until crisp—sprinkled with some salt and you have chicken cracklings! Chicken can be cooked for long periods, braised in wine, roasted, deep-fried, shallow-fried, poached in soothing broths, cooked and eaten cold, or dressed in creamy sauces. It can be casseroled, curried, and cured.

In this chapter, I've tried to live up to this trailer by sharing five very different methods of cooking chicken. I don't want to hear that it's boring again!

Roast Chicken, Parsnips, & Garlic

Delicious, succulent, garlicky chicken. Poaching the bird before you roast it makes it extra moist. Serve this with a generous dollop of Bread Sauce (see page 262).

Preheat the oven to 350°F.

Season the cavity of the chicken with salt. Place the chicken in a large, heavy-bottomed saucepan, add the bay leaves and the thyme, and pour over just enough water to cover the bird. Place the saucepan over high heat and bring to a boil. Remove immediately from the heat and leave the chicken to cool in the pan for 10 minutes. Then remove the chicken from the water. Drain all the liquid from the cavity and set the bird aside on a wire rack to drip dry.

While the chicken is drying, place a roasting pan in the oven to heat it—about 10 minutes. Season the chicken generously with salt and pepper and drizzle 1 tablespoon of the vegetable oil over the top. Place the parsnips and garlic in a bowl, season with salt and pepper, and add the remaining vegetable oil.

Remove the hot pan from the oven. Place the chicken in the middle of the pan and scatter the parsnips and garlic around it. Roast in the oven for 40–50 minutes, or until the chicken juices run clear.

Remove the chicken from the oven and set aside to rest for about 10 minutes. Don't cover it, or the skin won't stay crisp. Carve and serve with some greens on the side, dividing up the parsnips and garlic. And don't forget the Bread Sauce.

Serves 4

1 chicken, about 3½lb

salt and pepper

2 bay leaves

2 sprigs of thyme

2 tbsp vegetable oil

6 parsnips, peeled, quartered, and cored

1 head of garlic, broken into cloves

Braised Chicken Legs, Onion, & Bacon

Serves 4

4 large chicken leg portions, cut in half, with the thigh and drumstick separate

salt and pepper

3 tbsp vegetable oil, plus extra for seasoning

16 baby onions, peeled

2oz smoked bacon, cubed, or lardons

4oz small button mushrooms

2 sprigs of thyme

¾ cup red wine

2½ cups Chicken Stock (see page 259)

Chicken legs lend themselves to so much more than the barbecue. They roast and braise beautifully, and the meat stays nice and firm. They are affordable, too. I like to serve this dish with griddled baby leeks and a pile of mashed potatoes and celery root.

Preheat the oven to 325°F.

Season the chicken pieces with salt and pepper. Heat a heavy flameproof baking dish over medium heat. Pour in the vegetable oil and, once it is hot, seal the chicken pieces by turning them over once or twice in the baking dish, until golden brown all over. Remove from the baking dish and set aside.

Reduce the heat, add the baby onions, and cook, stirring gently for 4–6 minutes, until they start to color. Add the bacon, mushrooms, and thyme and cook for another 5 minutes. Add the red wine, allow it to bubble, and reduce the liquid by half.

Reintroduce the chicken to the dish and add some of the chicken stock so that it covers the chicken three-quarters of the way up—some of the skin should stay clear of the liquid to brown. Place in the oven for 40 minutes, or until the chicken is cooked through. Test the pieces with a skewer—the juices will run clear when the chicken is cooked.

If the sauce seems a little thin, remove the chicken and set it aside. Bring the sauce to a boil and let it reduce until it has a thicker consistency. Then put the chicken back in the sauce to keep it warm.

To serve, place a drumstick and thigh piece on each plate and surround with the sauce.

Whole Poached Chicken, Lemongrass, & Bok Choy

Serves 4–6

1 chicken, about 3½lb

salt and pepper

1 red chile, split down the middle

1 lemongrass stalk, crushed

3oz fresh ginger, peeled and thinly sliced

½ cup long-grain rice

4 heads of bok choy, trimmed and cut in half lengthwise

Sometimes I crave a really simple and clean-tasting dish—and it doesn't come much better than this. The lemongrass and ginger give the broth a tangy warmth, while the soothing chicken and rice make this the most comforting bowl of food. Don't forget to make the simple chile sauce in the tip if you like spice.

Season the cavity of the chicken with salt and pepper. Place the chicken in a large, heavy-bottomed saucepan with the chile, lemongrass, and ginger. Cover with cold water and bring to a boil. Simmer for 1 hour or so. To check whether the chicken is ready, test it with a skewer—the juices will run clear when it is cooked. Then remove the saucepan from the heat, check the seasoning, and set aside. Leave the chicken to cool in the liquid for 30 minutes.

Lift the chicken out of the broth and set it aside. Then pass the broth through a fine strainer into a clean saucepan.

Put the rice in another saucepan and cover it with ⅔ cup of the broth. Bring to a boil over high heat. As soon as it reaches a boil, reduce the heat, put on the lid, and allow to simmer for about 10 minutes, until the broth has been absorbed. Turn off the heat and set aside.

While the rice is cooking, remove all the chicken meat from the bone, trying to keep it in large chunks, and set aside.

Put the remaining broth back on the heat. Add the chicken and bring to a boil. Add the bok choy to the saucepan and cook for 2 minutes. Season to taste.

To serve, place the chicken, bok choy, and the broth in individual bowls and serve with the rice on the side.

BRYN'S TIPS
Here's a simple chile sauce that is fantastic with this dish. Process 5 chiles in a blender or food processor with 1 tablespoon sugar, 1 tablespoon soy sauce, and a splash of rice wine vinegar. Serve in a bowl on the side.

Pan-fried Chicken, Wild Garlic, & Wild Mushrooms

This dish reminds me of the flavors in an old-fashioned chicken Kiev. But there's no deep-frying here, and I've added some mushrooms because they go so well with chicken. Do try to use wild garlic, in season. It adds another dimension to the dish. But if you can't get it, or it is out of season, a mixture of garlic and parsley makes a perfectly acceptable substitute.

Preheat the oven to 325°F.

Season the chicken breasts with salt and pepper. Heat a heavy-bottomed, ovenproof frying pan and, when it is hot, add the olive oil. When that's hot, put in the chicken breasts, skin-side down. Cook until the skin is golden brown—don't be afraid to leave it for a while, at least 5 minutes.

Meanwhile, cook the potatoes in boiling salted water for 10 minutes, or until ready. Drain, then add the chopped chives. Set aside and keep warm.

Now, season the baby onions with salt, pepper, and a pinch of sugar. Turn the chicken breasts over and add the onions to the pan. Place in the oven and cook for another 7–8 minutes, or until the meat is cooked through and the juices run clear.

While the chicken and onions are in the oven, heat a nonstick frying pan. Add a pat of butter and, once it has melted, add the wild mushrooms. Season with salt and pepper and leave to cook for a minute or so, making sure all the liquid from the mushrooms has evaporated. Then add the chopped shallot and cook for another 2 minutes. Reduce the heat, add the cream, and bring to a boil. Once it is boiling, add the wild garlic (or garlic and parsley).

To serve, divide the mushroom mixture equally between four large bowls and place the chicken breasts on top. Scatter the onions over the top and serve with the new potatoes on the side.

Serves 4

4 chicken breasts, skin on

salt and pepper

2 tbsp olive oil

12 baby or new potatoes

1 tbsp finely chopped chives

3 baby onions, peeled and cut in half

pinch of sugar

¼ cup butter

4oz pied de mouton mushrooms (see tip, below)

1 shallot, peeled and finely chopped

⅓ cup heavy cream

6 leaves of wild garlic, finely shredded, or 1 tbsp each chopped garlic and parsley, mixed together

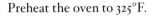

BRYN'S TIPS
I recommend pied de mouton mushrooms for this dish because they have plenty of flavor and hold their shape and texture well. But feel free to use any wild mushroom you like.

Chicken Liver Pâté

Makes 16 slices

½ cup port

½ cup Madeira

3 tbsp brandy

6 shallots, peeled
and finely sliced

sprig of thyme

1 garlic clove, peeled
and finely sliced

9oz foie gras, sliced

9oz chicken livers,
trimmed and chopped

1 tsp pink salt
(see tip, below)

1 tsp salt

black pepper

5 eggs

2¼ cups unsalted butter

You will need a
10 × 2 × 3in terrine dish,
lined with plastic wrap.

Whenever we put this on the menu at my restaurant it seems to be a huge draw. It's that good. If you can't get or don't want to use foie gras, don't worry. Just substitute some extra chicken livers and everything will work out. You'll need to start this the day before you want to serve it. I love it with crisp toast and Pear Chutney (see page 250).

Preheat the oven to 325°F.

Pour the port, Madeira, and brandy into a heavy-bottomed saucepan. Add the shallots, thyme, and garlic, and reduce over medium heat until the pan is almost dry. Set aside to cool. Once cold, refrigerate for at least 1 hour.

Place the foie gras and the chicken livers in a bowl. Add the cold port and Madeira mixture, the two salts, and the pepper, and mix together. Cover tightly with plastic wrap and set aside until everything reaches room temperature.

Crack the eggs into a bowl and cover. Melt the butter over low heat, and then set aside until it reaches room temperature. When all the ingredients have reached room temperature—which makes it easier for them to combine—blend the foie gras and chicken livers together in a blender or food processor. Add the eggs, then the butter, and blend again. Finally, pass the mixture through a fine strainer and pour into the lined terrine dish.

Place the terrine dish in a roasting pan, then pour warm water into the pan so that it reaches halfway up the side of the mold. This will help the pâté to cook evenly. Cover the terrine dish tightly with foil and bake in the oven for 45 minutes. Remove and set aside to cool.

When the pâté is cool, place it in the refrigerator overnight. The next day, remove the pâté from its mold, slice, and serve.

BRYN'S TIPS
If you can't find pink salt, don't worry. Any salt will do, and the taste will not be affected. But if you use regular salt, the pâté will be gray. Pink salt helps the liver to preserve its pinky color.

Beef

In our home, a classic roast dinner was beef. Beef with Yorkshire puddings, roast potatoes, and all the trimmings. Even today, I always make sure that there's a roast sirloin on the menu for Sunday lunch at the restaurant. But, back then, it wasn't just roast beef my Mam made. She'd also cook fantastic beef pot-pies, with crisp pastry toppings, and deep-flavored gravy. Cottage pies, too. All good, sustaining, home-cooked food.

My uncle's farm at Llanrhaeadr was primarily a dairy farm, but he also kept 20 or 30 head of beef cattle. While there isn't a huge difference between the two, some breeds of cattle lend themselves better to milk production and others to beef. And my uncle's lovely black-and-white Friesians were great milkers. You'd never dream of eating them!

Beef cows tend to be blockier and, well, meatier animals. And today, as more and more farmers reintroduce different breeds of cattle once again, we can enjoy the subtle variations in their meat. A Devon Red is that bit different from a Hereford or a Dexter, or from the popular Aberdeen Angus. I prefer to use the wonderful Welsh Black. It's a hardy, robust breed, which spends most of its year in the mountains, where it gets plenty of exercise. This is really important: if a cow just stands around, it will end up fat, whereas in a fit, healthy cow, the fat will marble through the meat, giving it texture and flavor.

But more important than breed or even in the quality of life an animal has on the farm is the way in which the meat is hung.

Hanging and dry-aging beef draws the excess water from the meat, and allows its natural enzymes to begin to tenderize it. You will notice a marked difference in the quality of beef that has been hung for 21 days or more. Its taste and texture are just better. You can see the difference, too. Well-hung beef is deeper in color than wetter, redder, younger meat. So I often hang mine for an extra few days to get the full depth of flavor. It also renders the meat beautifully tender.

Don't be afraid of more unusual cuts of beef. The dense and delicious beef cheek has a wonderful line of fat running through it. Braise it long and slowly until it becomes meltingly tender, and yet still retains its shape. One cheek should be enough to feed three to four people. Oxtail, too, is a fantastic morsel for long braises and stewing. You want to cook it down so it just falls off the bone. Brisket's another very cheap cut, this time from the belly of the cow. Salt it and cook it in stock for a few hours to make a delicious salt beef. Top round also offers great value for money, but make sure you ask your butcher for pieces no bigger than about a two pounds, otherwise it will take too long to cook and will turn far too tough.

A good butcher should be able to source quality beef for you and, if you build up a relationship, will help guide you to the best cut to suit your needs. Because, however you plan to cook it, the quality of your beef is so, so important. It should be a lovely dark red, marbled with creamy fat, which will render and keep the meat moist. Remember: fat is flavor.

Steak Tartare

*Serves 6 as an appetizer
or light lunch*

2 shallots, peeled and
finely chopped

2 tbsp ketchup

1 tsp Dijon mustard

1 tsp Worcestershire sauce

2 tbsp olive oil

2–3 drops of Tabasco sauce

salt and pepper

18oz sirloin steak, sinew
and fat removed and finely
hand-chopped

8 small gherkins,
finely chopped

1 tbsp capers, finely chopped

2 tbsp chopped parsley

6 raw egg yolks (optional)

This, the sushi of the meat world, is absolutely delicious. The secret, of course, is to choose the best quality beef you can, because the flavor matters. I like to serve this with a pile of crispy, thin, well-salted fries, but toast is fantastic, too.

Mix the shallots, ketchup, Dijon mustard, Worcestershire sauce, olive oil, and Tabasco sauce together in a bowl. Season with salt and pepper and set aside. Place the chopped sirloin in a bowl and set aside in the refrigerator to cool.

Just before serving, pour the shallot and ketchup mixture over the cold sirloin. Mix everything together well. Add the gherkins and the capers, and mix well again. Then add the parsley. Taste the mixture and adjust the seasoning if you feel it needs it.

Divide the mixture evenly into six metal rings on individual plates—you could use large, straight-edged cookie cutters—making sure to push the meat down firmly so that it holds its shape when you remove the rings to serve the dish. Alternatively, divide the meat into six equal mounds on the plates.

If you like, you can add a raw egg yolk on top of each one to finish the dish, and stir it in as you eat it.

Roast Rib-Eye Steak

This is the king of roasts, and the method is deceptively simple—in effect, like cooking two massive steaks. Because the recipe is so straightforward, you need the best quality beef you can find. I like to serve this with a Béarnaise sauce on the side; make a simple version by adding some chopped tarragon to the Hollandaise Sauce on page 261. I also like to pair it with the Almond Potatoes on page 49 and some roasted porcini mushrooms.

Serves 4–6

2 rib-eye steaks,
bone in, 18–22oz each

salt and pepper

vegetable oil

Preheat the oven to 350°F.

Season the beef generously with salt and pepper. Heat a large, heavy-bottomed frying pan or a heavy-bottomed roasting pan over high heat. When it is hot, add the vegetable oil, and then the steaks, until they are sealed well—about 3–4 minutes on each side. Do not rush this stage: the beef should be golden brown all over.

Put the steaks in the oven and roast for 10–12 minutes (to serve medium-rare). Remove from the oven and set aside to rest for 15 minutes before serving.

Beef & Onion Stew

Serves 4

3–4 tbsp vegetable oil

18oz beef shank, diced

4 medium carrots, peeled and diced

24 baby onions, peeled

⅓ cup red wine

⅓ cup port

1 tbsp tomato paste

2 quarts beef stock

6oz wild mushrooms, trimmed, washed, and dried

1 garlic clove, peeled and chopped

sprig of thyme

salt and pepper

If you didn't enjoy a beef and onion stew when you were growing up, you missed a treat. It's just so comforting. I like to serve this stew with quantities of creamy mashed potato. You could also top it with pastry to make a fantastic pie.

Preheat the oven to 275°F.

Place a heavy-bottomed flameproof baking dish over medium heat. Add a little of the vegetable oil and, when it is hot, add the diced beef. Fry the meat until it is golden brown and caramelized all over. If the baking dish is not big enough, you may have to do this in batches—give the meat room to fry, rather than steam. When all the meat is browned, remove it from the baking dish and set aside.

Put the diced carrots and baby onions into the pan, adding some more of the oil, if required, and cook for 2–3 minutes. Add the red wine and port, and deglaze the baking dish, letting it bubble up until you have a nice syrupy liquid. Add the tomato paste and cook for another 2–3 minutes.

Return the beef to the dish and stir to mix it together thoroughly with the vegetables. Pour the beef stock over the top and bring to a boil. Skim off any scum that floats to the surface. Add the wild mushrooms, the garlic, and thyme, and season with salt and pepper. Cover the stew, and cook in the oven for 1½–2 hours. Serve hot.

BRYN'S TIPS
You should be able to get beef shank from your butcher, but if you can't find it, any good cut of stewing beef will do.

Ox Tongue Salad with Parsley & Crispy Capers

Tongue is such an underused cut. That's a real shame, because it's economical, delicious, and—spiked with big flavors like the shallots and capers here—can be a real show-stopper. I like to serve this salad with a spoonful of the Beet Purée on page 20. You will need to start this dish the day before you serve it because of the cooking and refrigeration time.

Wash the ox tongue well in cold water. Rinse, and then place it in a large, heavy-bottomed saucepan. Add the onion, carrot, celery, thyme, star anise, and peppercorns. Cover the ingredients with water, then bring to a boil and simmer gently over low heat for 3 hours, or until the tongue is tender. Keep an eye on it—you may need to add cold water as you go along. The tongue should be just covered at all times.

When the tongue is tender, remove it from the liquid and set aside to cool a little. Then, while it's still warm, peel off the skin and the gristle with a small, sharp knife—it should come away quite easily. Discard the skin and gristly pieces, set the tongue aside to cool completely, then refrigerate for at least 3 hours, but preferably overnight.

Once the tongue is cold and firm, take a very sharp knife and slice it as thinly as possible. Set aside. Now, place the shallot rings in a glass bowl. Pour the lemon juice over the top and season with salt and pepper, to taste. Set aside to marinate for 20 minutes.

Finally, heat some oil in a deep-fat fryer to 356°F. Fry the capers in the oil—stand back, since they will spit like crazy—until they are golden and open like little flowers, about 30 seconds. Remove from the oil and drain on paper towels. If you're worried about the spitting or don't have a deep-fat fryer, leave out the capers. But they do add a lovely salty crunch to the dish.

To serve, overlap the slices of ox tongue on a platter and season with salt and pepper. Scatter the shallot rings and crispy capers over the top, and drizzle with the olive oil. Sprinkle the lemon zest and the garden cress over the top.

Serves 4–6 as an appetizer

1 small ox tongue

1 onion, peeled and chopped

1 carrot, peeled and chopped

1 celery stick, trimmed and chopped

sprig of thyme

1 star anise

5 peppercorns

2 shallots, peeled and thinly sliced into rings

juice and zest of 1 lemon

salt and pepper

vegetable oil, for deep frying

2 tbsp capers, drained well and patted dry

1 tbsp olive oil

garden cress, to scatter

Braised Oxtail, Turbot, & Cockles

Serves 4

18oz oxtail, chopped

1 large onion, peeled and chopped

1 large carrot, peeled and chopped

2 bay leaves

2½ cups red wine

3 tbsp vegetable oil

½ cup all-purpose flour

salt and pepper

2 quarts Chicken Stock (see page 259)

14oz cockles, cleaned (discard open ones)

½ cup white wine

1 tbsp olive oil

1oz samphire (or glasswort, if unavailable)

pinch of grated nutmeg

juice of 1 lemon

4 pieces of turbot, about 4½oz each, skinned

¼ cup butter

2 tbsp crème fraîche

This is based on the dish that won me the BBC's Great British Menu competition in 2006, and which was served at Her Majesty The Queen's 80th birthday banquet. There are quite a few components to this recipe, so read it through carefully before you begin. You will need to start at least a day ahead.

Put the oxtail into a large, heavy-bottomed saucepan with the onion, carrot, bay leaves, and red wine and set aside to marinate for 24 hours.

The next day, remove the oxtail and the vegetables with a slotted spoon and place on separate plates. Set aside the red-wine marinade in its saucepan. Preheat the oven to 275°F. Place the pan of marinade on the heat and bring to a boil. Reduce to a quarter of the volume. Skim off any scum or foam that rises to the surface. Take off the heat and set aside. Heat a heavy-bottomed flameproof baking dish and add 1 tablespoon of vegetable oil. Season the flour and use it to dust the oxtail. When the oil is hot, add the oxtail pieces, allowing each one to color until golden brown all over. Remove the browned meat and set aside. Add the marinated vegetables to the baking dish and fry until golden brown. Pour in the red wine marinade and deglaze the baking dish, allowing it to bubble until the liquid has reduced by half. Now, return the oxtail to the dish. Cover with the stock and bring to a boil. Skim again, removing any excess fat or scum. Place in the oven for 2½ hours, until the meat is falling off the bone. Set aside to cool in the liquid. When the oxtail is completely cool, remove it from the liquid and pick the meat from the bones, trying to keep it in large pieces. Strain the liquid through a fine strainer into a clean saucepan and bring to a boil. Simmer until reduced by half to make an oxtail jus. Then remove from the heat, set aside, and keep warm.

Put the cockles into a large, warmed saucepan with the white wine. Cover and cook on high heat for 1–2 minutes, or until the shells have opened. Discard any that remain closed. Strain through a colander, reserving the liquid. Pick the cockles out of their shells and set the meat aside to keep warm.

In another saucepan, warm the olive oil. Add the samphire (or glasswort), nutmeg, salt, pepper, and lemon juice. Cook for 30 seconds, then remove from the heat. Set aside. Place a nonstick pan over medium heat. When hot, add the remaining oil. Place the turbot into the pan and cook until the underside has browned (2–3 minutes). Turn the pieces over and cook for 2–3 minutes over reduced heat. Add the butter to finish the cooking.

Divide the oxtail between the plates and arrange the samphire and cockles on top. Drizzle with oxtail jus. Place a piece of turbot on the side. Bring the cockles cooking liquid to a boil and whisk in the crème fraîche. Pour over the oxtail and serve.

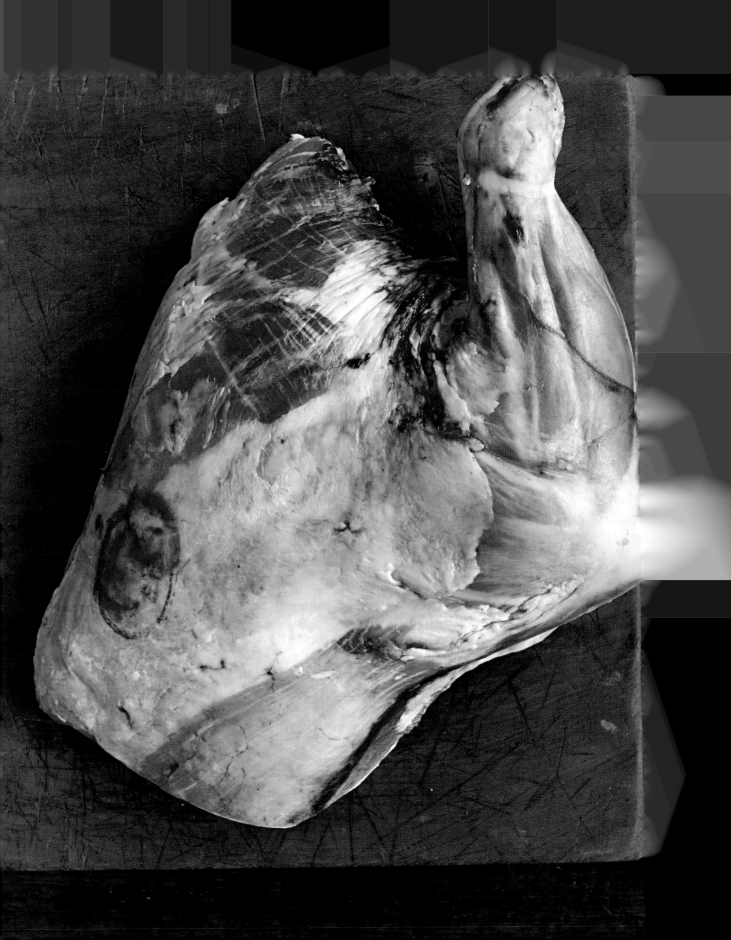

Lamb

Coming from Wales, I couldn't write a book without mentioning lamb, now, could I? But it's not just about my heritage; lamb really is a favorite of mine. I grew up surrounded by sheep, and they meant a lot to my family and to the local economy. Both my uncles kept lamb on their land. Uncle Gareth had something like 5,000 head of sheep—that's a heck of a lot of lambs come lambing time! My cousins' abiding memory is of bottle-feeding some of the smaller lambs by the Aga stove in the kitchen on cold evenings. That was real animal husbandry, up close and personal.

Lamb was part of our staple diet—all the cuts used and nothing wasted. What we didn't eat was sold or bartered. It's a regular on the menu at the restaurant, too. We tend to start the year cooking with mutton, which, contrary to popular belief, is not an old sheep, but a more mature lamb. I love its deep flavor and dense texture, and I do wish more people would buy it and enjoy it. We then move on to the new season's lamb, sweet and giving, and usually milk-fed, before rounding off the year with salt-marsh lamb, which has grazed on the briny estuary marshes, eating samphire and sea lavender, and has an intense flavor.

They are all fantastic products. Not one of them is better than the other: they're just different.

I get three or four whole lambs delivered to the restaurant every week, directly from Wales, and we butcher them ourselves. The legs are superb for roasting—try to keep them nice and pink. Shoulder is a fattier cut and good for long, slow cooking. Neck fillet is great for braises, chops for broiling and frying. We confit lamb, we poach it, make stock from it, roast it—in fact, we use every part of it.

We do a loin of mutton with a shepherd's pie on the side. The kidneys are deviled and served with toast, and the liver is served alongside chops. Braised heart with smoked bacon is a real favorite. We roast the bones for a good brown stock, and we even render the fat to add to stews and gravies. It has so much lamby flavor; try frying your chops in it, and you'll see what a difference it makes. You name it—nothing goes to waste. That's the old philosophy kicking in: respect the creature and make use of as much of it as you can. As always, buy the best quality you can afford—you will notice the difference.

Slow Roasted Shoulder of Lamb

Serves 4–6

1 small shoulder of lamb,
about 3½– 4½lb

salt and pepper

3 tbsp vegetable oil

½ cup unsalted butter

2 onions, peeled and sliced

sprig of rosemary,
leaves roughly chopped

5 large potatoes,
peeled and sliced

1 quart lamb stock

1 garlic bulb

You will need a heavy-
duty roasting pan, about
10 × 14in, plus a wire rack
that will fit over it.

Shoulder tends not to be used as much as leg of lamb, and
I think that's a shame. This succulent, slightly fatty joint
cooks down to a moist, tender, melting mass of flavor.
And the accompanying potatoes are to die for.

Preheat the oven to 250°F.

Season the shoulder of lamb generously with salt and pepper. Heat the vegetable oil
gently in a heavy-bottomed frying pan. Place the lamb in the pan and slowly allow it to
color, turning it until it is golden brown all over. Remove the lamb from the pan and
set aside.

Wipe any leftover oil from the frying pan with paper towels, then place the pan back on
the heat. Add the butter. When it has melted, add the sliced onions and cook gently for
10–15 minutes, or until golden brown. Add the chopped rosemary, stir well to combine,
then remove the pan from the heat and set aside.

Lay some of the potato slices on the bottom of the roasting pan, season with salt and
pepper, and then add a layer of golden-brown onion. Add a second layer of potatoes,
then more onion, and a final layer of potatoes. The height of the potato and onion stack
should be about 2in.

Pour the lamb stock over the top layer of the potatoes until it just covers them. Cut the
garlic bulb in half horizontally, and place it on top of the potato and onion stack.

Place the wire rack over the potato and onions, and put the lamb on top. Put the whole
thing into the oven and leave to cook slowly for 5–6 hours, or until the meat is really
tender. All the delicious lamb juices will soak into the potatoes and the lamb stock will
evaporate, leaving a sweet mixture of onion and potato.

To serve, shred the lamb off the bone, and serve with the potatoes, dividing up the garlic
equally. I like to serve this with a simple green salad.

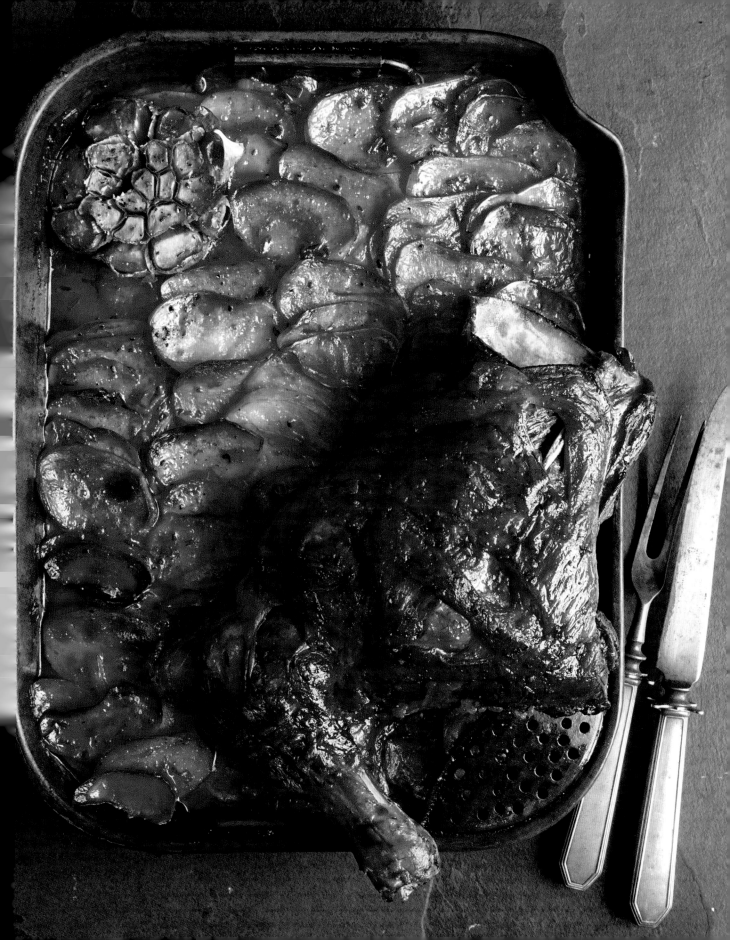

Mutton & Rutabaga Pie

Mutton is such an underused meat. People assume it comes from an old animal, but that's not true—the lamb is just a bit more mature. The meat has a fantastic flavor, so do make an effort to seek it out for this homey, tasty, satisfying pie.

Preheat the oven to 350°F.

Tie the rosemary, bay leaves, thyme, and celery together with string to make a bouquet garni and set aside.

Season the diced mutton with salt and pepper. Heat a heavy-bottomed saucepan on the stove and, when it is hot, add the olive oil. Fry the mutton until golden brown all over. If the pan is small, you may have to do this in batches. Remove the browned mutton from the pan and set aside.

Now reduce the heat, add the diced rutabaga to the saucepan, and cook until it caramelizes. Remove from the pan and set aside. Add the celery and onion and cook until soft. Then pour in the Madeira and allow it to reduce by half.

Return the mutton and rutabaga to the pan and cover with the stock. Bring the pan to a boil, skimming off any excess fat that rises to the surface. Add the bouquet garni and cook for 1 hour, or until the mutton is tender. Taste the sauce and adjust the seasoning, if necessary. Pour into the pie dish, removing the bouquet garni, and set aside to cool.

Now, using a piping bag with a large nozzle, carefully pipe an even layer of the mashed potato over the surface of the meat. Bake the pie in the oven for about 20 minutes, until it is golden brown and piping hot in the center. Serve with your choice of vegetables.

Serves 4–6

For the bouquet garni

sprig of rosemary

2 bay leaves

sprig of thyme

1 celery stick

For the pie

14oz mutton shoulder, diced

salt and pepper

1 tbsp olive oil

1 medium rutabaga, peeled and chopped into cubes the same size as the mutton

1 celery stick, trimmed and chopped

1 onion, peeled and chopped

⅔ cup Madeira

1 quart mutton or lamb stock

18oz potatoes, peeled, boiled, and mashed

You will need a 10in pie pan and a piping bag with a large nozzle.

Lamb Stew with Rosemary Dumplings

Serves 4

1lb 7oz lamb for stewing, cubed

salt and pepper

1 tbsp all-purpose flour

2 tbsp olive oil

12 baby onions, peeled

2 medium carrots, peeled and cut into ¾in cubes

1 medium rutabaga, peeled and cut into ¾in cubes

1¾ cups white wine

2½ quarts lamb stock

4 bay leaves

2 sprigs of rosemary

1 tbsp chopped parsley

For the dumplings

1 cup all-purpose flour

3oz suet

pinch of salt

½ tsp baking powder

1 tbsp chopped rosemary

I grew up eating stews like this. I've given this one a twist by adding rosemary to the dumplings, but feel free to substitute any other herb. As the name suggests, stewing meat is perfect for stews, and it's economical, making this a great-value winter dinner.

Preheat the oven to 250°F.

Season the lamb with salt and pepper and dust it lightly with the flour. Heat a heavy-bottomed flameproof baking dish and, when it is hot, add the olive oil and fry the lamb until golden brown. You may have to do this in batches so that you don't overcrowd the pan and to ensure that the meat browns evenly. Remove the lamb from the baking dish with a slotted spoon and set aside.

Reduce the heat, add the onions, carrots, and rutabaga to the baking dish and fry for 3–4 minutes, or until the vegetables are caramelized and sticky. Add the wine and simmer until reduced by half. Now add the browned lamb and enough of the lamb stock to cover the meat. Bring to a simmer and add the bay leaves and rosemary. Cover the baking dish with a lid and place in the oven for 1 hour.

While the lamb is cooking, mix all the dumpling ingredients in a large bowl, adding enough cold water to form a sticky dough. Then flour your hands well and roll the dough into 12 little balls. Place in the fridge to chill for 20 minutes or so.

Bring the remaining lamb stock to a boil in a large saucepan and poach the dumplings for 6–8 minutes, or until doubled in size. Remove them from the stock with a slotted spoon and set aside to rest. Discard the stock.

When the lamb stew is ready, remove the lid and add the dumplings to the baking dish along with the chopped parsley. Serve in shallow bowls, dividing up the dumplings evenly.

Bryn's Tips
Suet is the solid, white fat found around the kidneys and loins of beef and sheep. It's used in many traditional British recipes, but can be hard to come by in the US. Your best bet is to find a good, local butcher who sells suet, or to ask at the meat counter of your grocery store. In terms of flavor, there really is no substitute for suet, but if you come up short in your search, you can use an equal amount of solid vegetable shortening instead, as it has a similar melting point to suet. Butter has a lower melting point, so substituting butter for suet can make a recipe taste greasy.

Roast Rump of Lamb & Spice-scented Pearl Barley Broth

My Mam made big, hearty, warming lamb stews like this when I was growing up. I adored them and loved the way she used pearl barley to thicken the broth. There was always some in the pantry on the farm—it fed the pigs, the lambs, and us! The Asian-influenced herb and spice combination here is fresh and vibrant, bringing a traditional dish right up to date. So this is a dream supper dish for me: one big bowl of happiness.

Preheat the oven to 350°F.

Rinse the leek well under cold running water, then thinly slice the white and the tender light-green leaves.

Heat 1 tablespoon of the olive oil in a heavy-bottomed saucepan and gently sweat the garlic, celery, rutabaga, celery root, and leek. Add the star anise, cloves, and cinnamon stick. When the vegetables have softened, add the chicken stock and the pearl barley. Season with salt and pepper and bring to a boil. Reduce to a simmer over low heat for 30–40 minutes, or until the barley is just tender. You may need to add a little more stock or water if the barley is still firm.

Place a heavy-bottomed frying pan with a metal handle over medium heat. Once it is hot, add the remaining olive oil. Season the lamb with salt and pepper, place it fat-side down in the pan, and leave it to color—it needs to be nicely brown. Turn the lamb over to brown the other side well before turning it back onto its fat side. Put it into the oven for 8–10 minutes, to render the fat. When the lamb is ready, remove it from the pan and set aside to rest for 20 minutes.

To serve, heat up the stock and barley mixture and finish it by adding the chopped herbs. Add the bok choy leaves and drizzle the sesame oil over the top. Pour into deep plates. Slice each lamb rump into four and place on top of each plate.

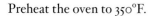

BRYN'S TIPS
Lamb rump is a beautiful piece of meat from the top of the lamb's leg—your butcher can cut this for you. In the US, it is usually called top round. If you can't find it, feel free to use a rump steak, but choose a thick one that will stay pink in the middle when nicely browned on the outside.

Serves 4

1 leek, trimmed and cut in half

2 tbsp olive oil

1 garlic clove, peeled and finely chopped

4 celery sticks, peeled and cut into ¼in dice

1 small rutabaga, peeled and cut into ¼in dice

1 small celery root, peeled and cut into ¼in dice

1 star anise

2 cloves

1 cinnamon stick

2 cups Chicken Stock (see page 259)

½ cup pearl barley

salt and pepper

4 lamb rumps, about 6oz each

handful of chervil, mint, and chives, finely chopped

2 small bok choy, trimmed and leaves separated

1 tbsp sesame oil

Roast Loin of Lamb, Peas, Lettuce, & Bacon

Serves 4

2 loins of lamb, weighing 1¼lb in total

salt and pepper

2 tbsp vegetable oil

2 strips of smoked bacon, diced

1 onion, peeled and diced

2 cups lamb stock

⅔ cup peas, cooked

¼ cup butter

1 Little Gem lettuce, shredded

sprig of mint

A tender loin of lamb with a classic combination of peas, lettuce, and bacon makes a perfect spring meal.

Preheat the oven to 325°F.

Season the lamb well with salt and pepper. Place a heavy-bottomed frying pan with a metal handle over medium heat. When it is hot, add 1 tablespoon of the vegetable oil. Put the lamb into the pan and color it all over, turning it so that all the sides brown evenly. Don't rush this—the dish will have much more flavor and color if you take your time. Place the lamb in the oven for 8–10 minutes. Remove the lamb from the oven, take it out of the frying pan, and set aside to rest for 10–15 minutes.

In another frying pan, add the remaining vegetable oil and cook the bacon over medium heat until crisp and golden. Add the onion and cook for another 2 minutes. Cover the bacon and onion with lamb stock and bring to a boil. Add the peas, the butter, the lettuce, and the mint, and season with salt and pepper to taste, then immediately remove from the heat.

To serve, slice the lamb, pour the pea and bacon mixture into a large bowl or individual serving dishes, and arrange the lamb slices on top.

Pork

My uncle always kept pigs on the farm and, let me tell you, those pigs ate like kings! Any apples or vegetables we didn't sell went straight to the pigs. Any cream or buttermilk the dairy didn't take—yep—the pigs got that, too. These were the happiest, healthiest pigs in North Wales. They were also a staple of the farm, giving back far more than they received.

One of my most vivid memories is of a pork carcass hanging up in the barn. Nain would point at the pig with her knife and ask us, "What do you want for dinner? You can have this bit or that bit." Then, when we had made our choice, she would climb onto a stool and carve off the piece, cart it into the kitchen, and cook it simply and beautifully. It never occurred to us, at that young age, to ask why the cuts we were offered started from the bottom of the beast and ended with the cheeks or head. Nain is a small woman and we got whatever cut she could reach perched on that stool! So we ate from hock to head, end to end. It taught me what a versatile meat pork is, and how much of the animal we can and should use. Pork isn't just about chops and roasts—there's ham, blood sausage, head cheese, terrines, pig's feet, cheeks, ears, and crispy tails. And who doesn't jump for joy at the mere sound of crackling cracking?

The pig lends itself to all manner of delights. Sweet, salty, smoky bacon offers a trio of crispy pleasure. Pork belly—a truly sensational cut that is often ignored—takes time and patience, but has something very sexy about it, with its layers of sweet fat and gently giving meat. The pig's feet are wonderful added to stocks and soups, thickening them with natural gelatin. Pork shoulder is great cut into chunks and stews: there's a nice fat content there to keep the meat moist. At my restaurant, we cook the ears in some apple juice, then chop them and deep-fry them into delectable appley pork scratchings. We make rillettes from the trimmings, cooking them with duck fat. You name it—everything is used but the oink.

We're lucky nowadays that more and more rare-breed pork has come onto the market. In addition to the more famous Tamworths and Gloucestershire Old Spots, we also have the Welsh, a lovely lop-eared variety that was almost driven to extinction by commercial farming. Now, the breed is back from the brink, and I try to use as much of it, farmed free-range, as I can. It has a magnificent flavor.

These recipes are blueprints, from which you can build your own dishes. Adapt them as you will. But whatever you do, source the best meat you possibly can. The pig deserves it.

Bacon & Tomato Sandwich

What could be more simple than a bacon sandwich, served warm and crisp and oozing homemade Ketchup? This is my version, which is a real household favorite on a Saturday morning. Don't be scared of the duck fat—it will make bacon like you've never tasted before!

Lightly toast the bread, making sure you don't overcook it and make the slices too dry.

Heat the duck fat in a heavy-bottomed frying pan and fry the bacon until golden and crispy. Remove the bacon from the pan and set it aside to drain on paper towels for a minute.

Butter the toast, place the bacon on four of the slices, and top with the tomato. Season with salt and pepper and drizzle the Ketchup over the top. Cover with the remaining pieces of toast. Eat!

BRYN'S TIPS
Duck fat is an example of how good it is to use the whole animal. When you roast a duck, keep draining off the oil as you go—you'll be amazed at its thick, white creaminess as it cools. Store it in a sealed jar in the refrigerator to use when required. Duck fat makes the crispest roast potatoes and is also good for confiting—preserving cooked meat in fat.

Serves 4

8 thin slices of
sourdough bread

1 tbsp duck fat

24 strips of bacon—
the best you can find

butter

4 plum tomatoes, sliced

salt and pepper

Ketchup
(see page 262)

Crispy Blood Sausage, Poached Hen's Egg, & Fresh Peas

Serves 4

4 fresh eggs

1 tbsp white wine vinegar

salt and pepper

⅓ cup Chicken Stock
(see page 259)

¼ cup butter

1 cup fresh or frozen
peas, cooked

3½oz pea shoots or
garden cress

For the blood sausage

6oz blood sausage,
peeled and divided into
4 equal pieces

1 tbsp all-purpose flour

1 egg, beaten

½ cup bread crumbs

vegetable oil, for
deep frying

This is hugely popular with those who've had a "good Saturday night," shall we say! Don't be afraid of blood sausage. Blood sausage is an ode to the pig—an example of my philosophy of not wasting any part of an animal. This dish is not just for breakfast; it makes a great supper or light lunch, too.

If you have a deep-fat fryer, set it to 338°F. If not, preheat the oven to 350°F. Crack the eggs into four individual tea cups or small ramekins.

Bring a medium-sized pan of water to a rolling boil, adding the vinegar and 1 teaspoon salt. One by one, add the eggs. They will sink to the bottom of the pan and, as they do, watch the white come up and around the yolk. After about 30 seconds, the eggs will rise through the water again. At this point, scoop them out with a slotted spoon and immediately put them in a bowl of iced water to stop them from cooking. When the eggs are cold, remove them from the water with a slotted spoon, and set aside. Neaten them up by carefully trimming away any straggly bits of white with a pair of scissors.

Form the blood sausage into balls and dust them with the flour. Dip them into the beaten egg and, finally, roll them in the bread crumbs until thoroughly coated. Put on a plate and set aside.

Bring the chicken stock to a boil in a pan and bubble until the liquid is reduced by half. Add the butter and the cooked peas. Season to taste with salt and pepper. Take off the heat and put a lid on to keep warm.

If you're using a deep-fat fryer, deep-fry the blood sausage balls until golden brown, 2–3 minutes. Remove from the oil carefully, and set aside to drain on paper towels. If you do not have a deep-fat fryer, heat 2 tablespoons vegetable oil in a frying pan with a metal handle and fry the blood sausage balls until golden brown, moving them all the time so that they color evenly. This should take a few minutes. Then put them into the preheated oven to finish for 7–10 minutes. Remove carefully from the pan, and set aside to drain on paper towels.

Bring a pan of water to a boil, add the cooled eggs using a slotted spoon, and give them 30–60 seconds to heat through.

To serve, place a spoonful of peas and some of their broth into individual bowls, put the poached eggs on top, gently position the blood sausage on top of that and finish with a liberal sprinkling of the pea shoots or garden cress.

Pork

Slow Roasted Pork Belly with Chickpeas

Serves 4–6

2¼lb pork belly in one piece

4 tbsp olive oil

salt and pepper

1 small onion, peeled and finely chopped

1 tsp smoked paprika

6 plum tomatoes, peeled, deseeded, and chopped

15½oz can of chickpeas, drained and rinsed

⅔ cup Chicken Stock (see page 259)

2 tbsp finely chopped parsley

Pork belly has got to be one of my favorite cuts. It needs a little love and patience, but the end result is worth it. As for chickpeas, they're a real pantry staple in my kitchen and act as fat little sponges when cooked, soaking up every last drop of flavor. I recommend that you cook and refrigerate the pork belly the day before you plan to serve this dish.

Preheat the oven to 275°F.

Rub the pork belly thoroughly with 2 tablespoons of the olive oil, then season well with salt and pepper. Place the pork in a good-sized roasting pan and put it in the oven for 5–6 hours, until melting and tender.

Remove from the oven and place the pork in a clean roasting pan. Place another pan on top of the pork and weight it down—I often use cans from the pantry—to preserve the shape of the meat. Let it cool, then put the pan into the refrigerator until the pork is completely cold.

When it is cold, remove the skin from the pork belly and discard. Then cut the belly into slices 1in thick and set aside.

In a heavy-bottomed saucepan, heat 1 tablespoon of the olive oil and cook the onion until softened, without letting it color. Add the smoked paprika and cook for another 2–3 minutes. Then add the tomatoes and cook gently for another 5 minutes. Finally, add the drained chickpeas, cover with the chicken stock, and bring to a boil. Season with salt and pepper, and simmer until the stock has thickened and is coating the chickpeas. Then stir in half the chopped parsley.

Season the slices of pork belly with salt and pepper. Now heat the remaining tablespoon of olive oil in a frying pan over medium heat and fry the pork slices gently, until golden brown on both sides.

To serve, spoon the chickpeas into four large bowls, place the pork belly slices on top, and sprinkle with the remaining parsley.

Pork Cutlet, Fava Beans, Wild Mushrooms, Sage, & Apple

Pork chops are a delicious and economical cut. But how often do you find them dry and a bit tasteless? By asking your butcher to leave the two "chops" joined up, you not only get more meat for your money (it won't shrink and dry out), but you also gain a succulent and sweet piece of pork that's easier to cook. As for the dish itself: pork, apple, sage, beans with a few wild mushrooms to finish it off—it's the countryside on a plate.

Preheat the oven to 325°F.

Blanch the fava beans in plenty of boiling salted water for 1 minute, then plunge them immediately into iced water to stop them from cooking. Remove the skins and set side.

Season the pork with salt and pepper. Heat the olive oil and ¼ cup of the butter in a large flameproof baking dish and brown the pork all over, until golden and caramelized. Remove the pork and set aside.

Add the carrot and onion to the baking dish and cook for 2 minutes, then add the sage stalks. Return the pork to the baking dish, on top of the vegetables, and put it in the oven for 20 minutes. When it is ready, remove the pork from the baking dish and set aside to rest in a warm place.

Discard the onion and the carrot. Place the baking dish over medium heat and add another ¼ cup of the butter. Add the shallots and the sage leaves, and cook until soft. Add the mushrooms and cook until they are soft, too, then add the chopped apples. Cover everything with chicken stock, bring to a boil, and season with salt and pepper. Don't let it boil for too long—the apples should have some bite.

Add the remaining butter to the sauce to thicken it and make it glossy, and finish by adding the fava beans and heating them through. To serve, pour the fava bean, mushroom, sage, and apple mixture into two deep plates. Divide the cutlet into two chops with a sharp knife and place one on top of each plate.

Serves 2

18oz fava beans, podded

1 large pork cutlet with 2 bones in (i.e., 2 chops joined together)

salt and pepper

1 tbsp olive oil

¾ cup butter

1 medium carrot, peeled and chopped

1 medium onion, peeled and chopped

a bunch of sage, leaves and stems separated and chopped

2 shallots, peeled and chopped

7oz wild mushrooms

2 Cox's apples (or other dessert apple), peeled, cored, and chopped

¾ cup Chicken Stock (see page 259)

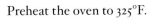

BRYN'S TIPS
Different varieties of apple cook at different rates, so keep an eye on the chopped apples in the baking dish and don't allow them to cook for too long.

Braised Pork Cheeks with Ginger Carrots

Serves 2

8 pork cheeks, trimmed

salt and pepper

2 tbsp olive oil

1 onion, finely chopped

6–8 garlic cloves, peeled and finely chopped

1 carrot, peeled and finely chopped

sprig of thyme

1 tsp coriander seeds, crushed

¾ cup ginger beer (or ginger ale if you can't find beer)

1 quart Chicken Stock (see page 259)

For the ginger carrots

18oz baby carrots, left whole with the green tops on

1 tbsp honey

1 tsp ground ginger

1½ tbsp butter

How can I describe pork cheeks? Two gems! Some people rave about the chicken's "oysters"—the tasty hidden pieces of meat—well, these are the porky version. They have lots of flavor, and are lean, but with just enough fat running through to make them succulent. Everyone has eaten them before—in the guise of a sausage. Now's the time to let them shine for themselves. And this is a great way to cook such an underused part of this magnificent animal.

To cook the pork cheeks, first season them with salt and pepper. Heat 1 tablespoon of the olive oil in a heavy-bottomed pan and fry the cheeks gently until golden on both sides—this should take only about 30 seconds per side if the pan is hot enough. Don't overcook them. Remove from the pan and set aside.

Add the remaining oil to the pan and, over medium heat, cook the onion, garlic, carrot, thyme, and crushed coriander seeds until golden brown, 2–3 minutes. Pour in the ginger ale and allow it to bubble until reduced to a syrupy glaze. Return the cheeks to the pan, placing them on the bed of vegetables. Add the chicken stock, bring to a boil, and simmer for about 1 hour. Leave to cool.

When the cheeks have cooled, remove them from the pan and set aside. Pass the braising liquor through a fine strainer into a clean pan and bring to a simmer. Reduce to a thick sauce—this should take 5 minutes or so—and taste for seasoning.

Put the cheeks back into the pan and glaze them all over. Take them off the direct heat, cover with a lid, and set to the side of the stove to keep warm.

Blanch the baby carrots in boiling salted water until tender. Drain, then plunge them into ice water to stop them from cooking. Drain again, dry the carrots, and set aside.

In a nonstick frying pan, bring the honey and the ground ginger very gently to a boil. Add the butter and the blanched carrots, and sauté for 1 minute, or until golden brown.

To serve, place the glazed cheeks and carrots on a plate, and pour any remaining sauce around them.

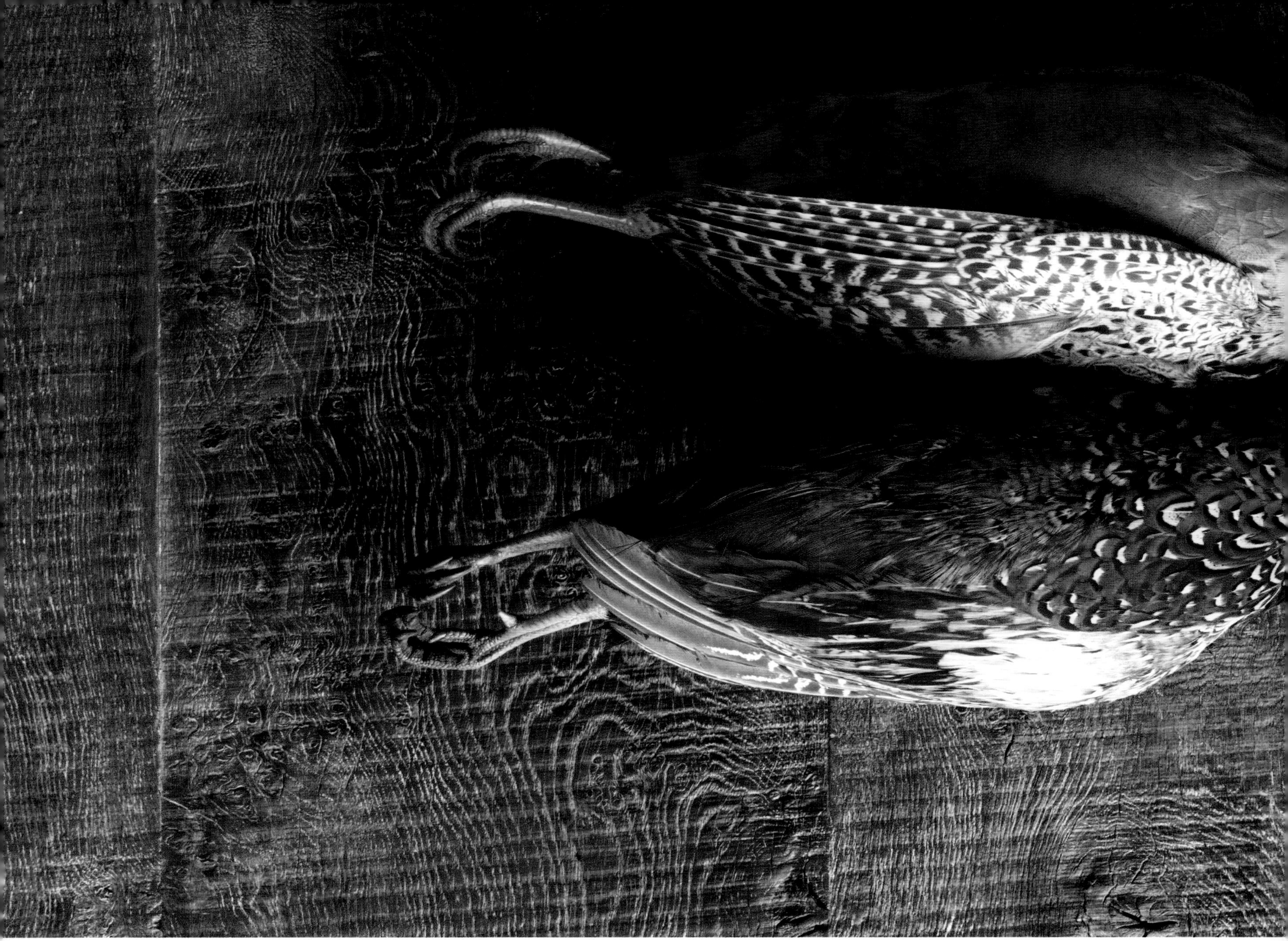

Game

Game

It's almost impossible to live on a farm without eating game. Free food sourced directly from the land is all around you, all the time. We'd go hunting regularly, often bartering the game we didn't eat with our neighbors—a couple of brace of pheasant in exchange for a basket of logs. Even today, my family supplies all the game birds we use at the restaurant.

Game is a terrific ingredient. Feathered or furred, there's a huge range of textures and flavors, it is plentiful, and stocks can be monitored easily, and it's a very healthy meat, too, being so low in fat. Its sustainability comes down to the management of stock, wild or not. I believe it's important to shoot only the game you need. If I require a dozen birds for the restaurant, for example, that's what I ask my suppliers to shoot—not 15 or 20. I learned that from my Dad and my uncles. It's wasteful and greedy to take more than you need. And damaging, too. If we destroy a game population, we destroy a vital part of our farmland ecology. We have not had hare on the menu for the last couple of seasons because the gamekeepers and farmers in North Wales had seen their stocks decline. They made an agreement not to shoot any more until they saw them improve. That is stewardhip in action. Hopefully, once stocks are up, we'll have them back on the menu again.

In this chapter, I want to illustrate the versatility of game. Mallard has always been one of my favorite wild ducks. It's rich and delicate at the same time, and very easy to source. Venison is the king of game, and has always been something of a luxury item. You can get terrific farmed venison now, but hunting wild deer takes real skill, so when I was a kid it was always hard to come by. Rabbit is a year-round ingredient, and absolutely delicious. I'm surprised people don't eat it more. It's cheap and easy to cook, you can use every bit of it, and the meat lends itself beautifully to all manner of cooking. Try to buy wild rabbit if you can—the taste and texture are superb. Pigeon (called squab when it's on the menu) is a fantastically versatile bird that takes flavor very well.

A final couple of notes: these are lean meats. On the one hand, this makes for good, healthy eating. On the other, it makes them prone to drying out during cooking. And remember—because these are wild, you can have two pheasants of the same size, shot on the same day in the same field, and one will feel, taste, and cook differently from the other. It depends on their age, how far they have flown, what they have eaten. So take care when you cook game to ensure it stays succulent and delicious. Then you'll enjoy some of the best meaty flavors the countryside can offer.

Game Terrine & Pear Chutney

Serves 4–6 as an appetizer

1½lb mixed game, ground

9oz pork belly, ground

2 eggs

1½oz dried apricots, chopped

1½oz pistachio nuts, shelled but kept whole

1 tsp fresh thyme leaves

salt and pepper

2 squab breasts, skinless

2 pheasant breasts, skinless

2 tbsp vegetable oil

10–12 slices of Bayonne ham

Pear Chutney (see page 250), to serve

You will need a 3 × 10in terrine dish, lined with plastic wrap.

Game can be a little dry, since it's very lean, but cooking it long and slowly with lovely fatty pork belly renders it moist and tender. This terrine makes a great appetizer or even a lunch dish, and Pear Chutney is the perfect accompaniment.

Preheat the oven to 250°F.

In a large bowl, mix the ground game and the ground pork belly together well. Add the eggs, chopped apricots, whole pistachio nuts, thyme leaves, salt, and pepper, and mix again. Set aside.

Season the squab breasts and the pheasant breasts with salt and pepper. Place a frying pan over high heat and, once it is hot, add the vegetable oil and then the breasts, allowing them to color on both sides. Remove the breasts from the pan, set aside to cool, and then place in the refrigerator until cold.

Line the terrine dish with the Bayonne ham, making sure that the slices overlap. Now spread one-third of the ground game mixture over the ham. Place a pheasant breast on top and a squab breast on top of that. Add another third of the ground game in a layer, then place the remaining squab and pheasant breasts on top. Finish with the final third of the ground game mix.

Fold the Bayonne ham over the last layer of ground game to seal the terrine, and then cover it with foil.

Place the terrine dish in a roasting pan, then pour warm water into the pan so that it comes halfway up the terrine. This will help it to cook evenly. Put in the oven for 2 hours. Then remove from the oven and allow to cool before refrigerating.

To serve, turn the terrine onto a plate. Slice it thinly, and serve with the Pear Chutney.

BRYN'S TIPS
Bayonne ham is an air-dried ham from southwest France. It has a slightly sweet and delicate flavor. If you can't find it, you can use bacon, or thin slices of prosciutto or pancetta, but do try to seek it out if you can.

Peppered Loin of Venison, Savoy Cabbage, & Celery Root

Serves 4

4 venison loin steaks, about 5½oz each

salt

2oz black peppercorns

1½ tbsp olive oil

4 tbsp duck fat

1 large carrot, peeled and cut into ¼in sticks

1 small celery root, peeled and cut into ¼in sticks

1 small Savoy cabbage, trimmed of dark outer leaves and shredded into ½in-wide ribbons

⅓ cup heavy cream

Venison, cabbage, celery root, and cream are all wonderfully seasonal ingredients. Don't be afraid of the quantity of pepper here. It helps to bring out the rich flavor of the meat.

Season the venison loins with salt, then roll each one in the crushed peppercorns until evenly covered.

Put the oil in a heavy-bottomed frying pan over medium heat. When it is hot, fry the pieces of venison for 3–4 minutes on each side, until the meat is firm to the touch, but springs back when you press it with your finger. It should stay pink in the middle. Remove from the pan and set aside in a warm place to rest.

Melt a third of the duck fat in a heavy-bottomed saucepan over medium heat. Add the carrot and celery root sticks and cook until tender. Strain the vegetable sticks through a colander, draining the fat into a heatproof bowl.

Return the saucepan to the heat, add the remaining duck fat and cook the shredded cabbage for a few minutes, until the ribbons begin to wilt slightly. Add the carrot and celery root sticks and cook for another 3–4 minutes. Strain the duck fat into a heatproof bowl. Return the pan to the heat and pour in the cream. Let it bubble slightly, until the cream lightly coats the cabbage leaves.

To serve, slice the venison and place on a large warm plate with the creamy cabbage to one side.

BRYN'S TIPS
The best way to judge the "doneness" of a steak—of any kind—is a simple touch test. With your right index finger, press the soft fleshy bit at the base of your thumb, keeping your thumb relaxed. The muscle should feel soft and squishy. That's the feel of rare meat. Now pull your thumb toward your palm and notice how the muscle becomes firmer and firmer. So does steak when you cook it. So a relaxed feel equates to a rare steak, a semifirm feeling to a medium steam, and a firm feel to a well-done steak. Practice this a few times and you'll be able to judge how well a piece of steak is cooked by feel alone. This is much more reliable than timings because every steak is different and cooks at a different speed.

Roast Mallard with Braised Red Cabbage & Game Fries

This was a regular supper when I was growing up. My Mam used to call it "free food." We had plenty of mallards on the river and lots of apples and red cabbage on the farm. These days, I like to serve it with game fries—they add a lovely crunch to the proceedings.

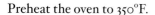

Preheat the oven to 350°F.

Season the mallard inside and out with salt and pepper. On the stove, heat a heavy-bottomed frying pan that can go in the oven or a heavy-bottomed roasting pan. When it is hot, add 1 tablespoon of the olive oil and then the mallard. Brown them, turning occasionally, until golden all over.

Place the ducks in the oven for 15 minutes, or until they are ready—they should remain pink in the middle. Remove from the oven, cover with foil, and set aside in a warm place to rest.

For the red cabbage, heat the olive oil in a heavy-bottomed saucepan. Add the onion, apple, and thyme and cook until just soft. Add the cabbage and cook until very tender.

Add the sugar, port, and red wine and let it bubble until it reduces to a lovely sticky glaze. Check the seasoning, and then finish off by stirring in the red currant jelly. Set aside and keep warm.

To make the game fries, peel the potatoes and slice them as thinly as possible—a mandolin is a great way of doing this. Dry the potato slices thoroughly and, if you have a deep-fat fryer, set the temperature to 284°F. Deep-fry the slices individually until golden. If you don't have a deep-fat fryer, heat a good amount of oil in a heavy-bottomed frying pan until very hot. Please be careful. Then fry the potatoes as above. Drain well on paper towels and season with salt.

To serve, remove the breasts and legs from the birds. Serve one breast and one leg per person, placing the meat on a warm plate on top of the cabbage. Garnish it with a pile of game fries.

Serves 4

2 mallard, gutted and dressed for roasting (ask your butcher or game dealer to do this)

salt and pepper

1 tbsp olive oil

For the red cabbage

3 tbsp olive oil

1 onion, peeled and sliced

2 apples, peeled, cored, and sliced

sprig of thyme

1 small red cabbage, finely shredded

¼ cup superfine sugar

½ cup port

½ cup red wine

4 tbsp red currant jelly

For the game fries

2 large Russet potatoes

oil, for deep-frying

Saddle, Shoulder, & Leg of Rabbit with Tomatoes, Olives, & Thyme

Serves 4

salt and pepper

1 rabbit, cut into saddle, shoulders, and legs (ask your butcher to do this)

3 tbsp olive oil

1 onion, peeled and finely sliced

a bunch of thyme (reserve 1 tbsp leaves)

1 tsp tomato paste

½ cup white wine

4 tomatoes, peeled, deseeded, and chopped

1¾ cups Chicken Stock (see page 259)

2 tbsp vegetable oil

12 baby onions, peeled

2 tbsp butter

4oz black olives, pitted

Rabbit can take big, bold flavors, so this is a warm, fragrant, slightly Mediterranean treatment. The sauce is so addictive that you'll want lots of bread to sop it up. The saddle is cooked separately from the shoulders and legs because it is more delicate and doesn't take as long to cook. So this method shows the rabbit's different textures and flavors at their best.

Preheat the oven to 350°F.

Season the rabbit legs and shoulders. Place a heavy-bottomed flameproof baking dish over medium heat. Heat half the olive oil, then sear the shoulder and legs on all sides until golden, being careful not to let them dry out. Remove from the pan and set aside.

Drain off the oil and wipe out the baking dish. Then pour in the remaining olive oil. Add the onion and cook until tender. Add the thyme, tomato paste, and wine, and cook for 2 minutes. Then add the chopped tomatoes. Place the rabbit shoulders and legs on top of the vegetables and cover with the stock. Bring to a boil. Cover with a lid and simmer gently for 30–40 minutes, until the rabbit is tender.

While the rest of the rabbit is cooking, season the saddle with salt and pepper. Place a frying pan with a metal handle over medium heat. Add 1 tablespoon of the vegetable oil and, when it is hot, put the saddle in the pan. Gently brown it all over for a few minutes—it should look golden and delicious. Put it in the oven for 8–10 minutes. Then remove the pan from the oven and set the rabbit aside to rest.

When the shoulder and leg pieces are tender, remove them from the heat and set aside, leaving the rabbit in the sauce for at least 30 minutes. Then remove the rabbit pieces from the baking dish, cover, set aside, and keep warm.

While the dish is cooling, pour the remaining vegetable oil into a frying pan over low heat. When it is hot, add the baby onions and cook, turning occasionally, until they are brown, then add the butter to finish the caramelization. This should take 5–6 minutes.

Pass the tomato sauce through a coarse strainer into a clean pan. Add the baby onions, the black olives, and the reserved thyme leaves, and bring back to a boil.

To serve, divide the legs, shoulders, and saddle into four portions, then spoon the sauce around the rabbit and serve with mashed potatoes.

Wood Pigeon, Fig Marmalade, Chocolate, & Vanilla Salt

I love the fact that the star ingredient in this dish is the simplest one—a beautiful wild bird. On a trip to Mexico about 10 years ago, I came across the exciting combination of chocolate and spices for the first time. I fell for it completely, hence this dish with one great inexpensive local ingredient given a modern edge with exotic additions.

Preheat the oven to 325°F.

Season the pigeon breasts with salt and pepper. Heat a heavy-bottomed frying pan with a metal handle over a fairly high heat, add the olive oil and then the breasts and let them color on both sides until golden brown. Transfer the breasts to the oven for 5 minutes, then take out and leave them to rest in a warm place—I think pigeon breasts should be served pink.

Break up the chocolate and melt it in a heatproof bowl over a saucepan of barely simmering water, making sure that the water does not touch the bowl, or the chocolate will burn. Let the chocolate melt slowly and then set aside, over the water, to stay warm.

To serve, using a pastry brush, paint the warm chocolate onto two plates and sprinkle over the garden cress and vanilla salt. Cut the pigeon breasts in half lengthwise and place half a breast on the chocolate. Spoon some fig marmalade on top and finish with the other half of the pigeon breast. Scatter garden cress over the top, and serve.

Serves 2

4 pigeon (squab) breasts, skinless

salt and pepper

2 tbsp olive oil

4oz good-quality dark chocolate, minimum 70 percent cocoa solids

4oz garden cress

1 tbsp vanilla salt

Fig Marmalade (see page 253), to serve

garden cress, to serve

Bryn's Tips
You can buy vanilla salt—I get mine from a local supplier—but if you can't find it easily, you can make it. Just put a vanilla pod into a jar of good sea salt and leave it for a few days. Look for local sea-salt suppliers, too, and find your favorite.

Apples

Of all of fall's fruit, apples are my favorite. There was an orchard near the farm, and a big apple tree at the house, so as kids we were never without them. In fact, you could say we had far too many. I have vivid memories of a huge gang of us boys trudging off to the river on fishing expeditions. There were apple trees all around, heavy with fruit. No matter how many fish we caught, the day would always end with us helping ourselves to the apples, followed by a huge apple fight. Opposing teams lined up on either bank, splashing in the water and letting fly with the apples. We'd get soaked and laugh until we almost couldn't breathe. And then, when we were done, I'd head home, sometimes with a fish or two, and always with an apple in my pocket. Looking back, it wasn't the best use for such great produce. But I was young and didn't know any better.

I think anyone who has grown up in apple country—no matter where in the world—will feel the same about these fruit. They take over your cooking and eating when they come into season, so at that time of year the kitchen smells sweet and spicy with baking or steaming apples. That scent always reminds me of home.

Apples are a wonderful ingredient. They go just as well with savory dishes as they do with sweet, they marry joyfully with pork and game, and there are hundreds of varieties to choose from, each with a taste or texture all its own. If you get the chance, experiment with different types. See what your local orchards are growing—the growers will be able to tell you which ones cook best in which ways, and introduce you to some you've never tasted before. And, by buying local apples, you do your bit to preserve rare varieties. They'll die out if nobody buys them because there will be no incentive to grow them.

I tend to use a lot of Braeburns in my cooking because they hold their shape well when they cook, without disintegrating. But if you have apples you prefer, use those instead. Cox's Orange Pippins make a great jelly, with their mixture of sweetness and acidity. I also like to use them for crumbles, since they break down nicely, but still keep some shape and texture. They are terrific mixed with damsons or berries. In the Apple Sorbet in this chapter, I insist on a Granny Smith. It colors the dish with such a striking and distinct pale green—it looks cool, as well as being a real palate cleanser after a rich meal.

I sometimes feel that we take apples for granted: they are a fantastic fruit. Try one of these recipes, or just try crunching into a juicy apple, straight from the tree.

Apple Sorbet

I love the fresh, clean flavors of this sorbet. It's a perennial favorite and incredibly simple to make. Serve it on its own, or on the side of a pie or tart. Note that I don't peel the apples, because the skin gives the sorbet a beautifully pale green color. If you don't have an ice-cream maker, follow the granita variation below, which makes a roughed-up, snowflake version of a sorbet.

First, make the simple syrup. In a heavy-bottomed saucepan, bring the water and the sugar to a boil, whisking all the time until the sugar dissolves. As soon as the syrup comes to a boil, remove it from the heat and allow to cool. When it is cold, place it in a covered container in the fridge—the syrup should be cold when you use it.

Place the apple pieces in a large bowl. Pour the simple syrup over them. Then, using a handheld blender, process the apples for 2–3 minutes, until smooth. Pass the mixture through a fine strainer into a clean bowl. Add the lemon juice, then either pour the mixture into an ice-cream maker or make a granita, as below. The sorbet should stay in the ice-cream maker for 20–25 minutes, or as long as directed in the manufacturer's instructions. Remove from the machine, transfer to a covered container, and store in the freezer until needed. It should keep for up to a week.

Variation: Apple Granita

Pour the prepared apple mixture into a fairly shallow container—a plastic container with a lid is ideal—and put it into the freezer for about 2 hours. (I put a metal fork in the freezer, too—you'll see why in a moment.) When the 2 hours are up, remove the lid. Look for the ice crystals forming around the outer edges of the container. With the chilled fork, mix these semifrozen parts inward, stirring them into the main body of the mixture. Put the lid back on and freeze for another 40 minutes or so, then repeat the forking process. You may have to do this two or three more times—it will take a good 4 hours in all—until you have a mass of snowy ice crystals that you can almost "fluff" with the fork. Keep covered in the freezer until needed.

BRYN'S TIPS

Simple syrup is a useful ingredient to have at home. Add a dash of liqueur or your favorite spirit, then use it to baste a sponge cake, to add to cocktails, or to confit fruit and vegetables. I use it to confit the cranberries in the Chocolate Chestnut Cake on page 202.

Serves 4

For the simple syrup

¾ cup water

⅔ cup superfine sugar

For the sorbet or granita

11oz Granny Smith apples, cored and chopped into small pieces

juice of 1 lemon

Baked Apples

Serves 4

4 Braeburn apples, cored and scored around the middle with a sharp knife

For the stuffing

¼ cup light brown sugar, packed

1 apple, grated

2oz golden raisins

2oz raisins

2 tbsp chopped almonds

juice and zest of 1 orange

1 tsp ground cinnamon

This is a real trip down memory lane for me. Cooking classes at school always included baked apple and I remember proudly carrying mine home to be tasted by the family. This one is a little more grown up, with spices and orange, but one whiff when it's cooking sends me back in time. This is such a simple recipe, so it's a great one to try with kids. You could serve it with custard or cream, but do try the Butterscotch Sauce on page 265.

Preheat the oven to 350°F.

Place the Braeburn apples on a baking sheet. Mix all the other ingredients together in a bowl and then, with a teaspoon, gently and evenly fill the cavity in each apple—where the core was—with the spiced fruit and nut mixture.

Bake the apples for 25–35 minutes, until they are soft (check by gently slipping the tip of a sharp knife into the side), slightly golden, and caramelized. Serve hot.

Apples

Apple Oat Granola Bars

Chewy, appley, oaty granola bars—I used to love them as a kid and have updated the recipe by adding some fresh apple. My Mam used to add gooseberries, too; anything that cuts against the sweetness of the golden syrup makes sense. These are perfect for picnics.

Preheat the oven to 325°F.

Place the butter, sugar, and golden syrup in a heavy-bottomed saucepan over low heat. Let them melt, stirring all the time until well combined. Add the grated apple and the oats and mix well.

Pour the mixture onto the prepared baking sheet and spread evenly, using the back of a spoon or a spatula. Bake for 10–15 minutes, or until golden.

Leave the granola bar mixture to cool for a few minutes on the baking sheet. Then remove the whole piece to a wire rack to cool. While it is still warm, mark it into squares with a knife. Let it cool completely, then break off the granola bar pieces. They should snap away cleanly where you've marked them.

Makes 12

1¼ cups butter

½ cup light brown sugar

3 tbsp golden syrup (or honey)

4oz peeled and grated apple

1½ cups rolled oats

You will need a 10 × 12in baking sheet, lined with parchment paper.

Spiced Apple & Chestnut Crumble

Serves 8

12 apples, peeled and cored

1 vanilla pod

⅔ cup superfine sugar

7oz cooked chestnuts

1 tsp ground apple pie spice

2 tbsp butter

For the crumble

2 cups all-purpose flour

1 cup superfine sugar

1 cup butter, straight
from the fridge

1⅓ cups sliced almonds

Crumble is reminiscent of home and comfort and Sunday lunch. I've made a few changes here by adding some spices and the gentle nuttiness of chestnuts. There's also a restaurant tip on how we keep crumble crunchy! Serve this with cream or the Vanilla Custard on page 266.

Preheat the oven to 325°F.

Cut three of the apples into small dice, then place in a heavy-bottomed saucepan with the vanilla pod and the sugar. Just cover the apples with water, and cook until soft. Depending on the variety, this should take 5 minutes or so—keep checking. Then break down the cubes with a fork until you have a rough mash. Set aside.

Cut the remaining apples and the chestnuts into bite-sized pieces, making them as uniform in shape as possible. Then season the apples and chestnuts with the apple pie spice.

Heat the butter in a heavy-bottomed frying pan, and fry the apple and chestnut mixture until you can smell the appley spiciness. Add to the mashed apples in the saucepan. Turn the heat back on under the saucepan and cook everything for another 10 minutes, or until all the chopped apples and chestnuts are cooked and soft. Take off the heat, remove the vanilla pod, and set aside.

To make the crumble, mix the flour and sugar together in a large bowl. Then add the butter in small pieces, rubbing it into the flour and sugar using the tips of your fingers until it has a crumbly texture, like rough bread crumbs. Add the sliced almonds and mix them through. Place the crumble mix on a baking sheet and cook in the oven until the mixture is golden brown, about 10 minutes. Baking it separately from the fruit ensures a good crispy crumble topping.

Spoon the cooked apple into individual ovenproof bowls or ramekins and cover evenly with the crumble mix. Bake in the oven for 10 minutes. Serve immediately with cream or custard.

Apple Tarte Tatin with Calvados Cream

I love apple pie, and this wonderful French version hits the spot every time, with its caramelization playing against the tartness of the apples. You could serve the tart on its own or with ice cream, but the Calvados Cream is simple to make, and adds another layer of appley flavor. It's best to start this the day before you plan to serve it, since the apples need chilling time.

Preheat the oven to 325°F.

Evenly cover the base of the frying pan with the butter—use your fingers to squash it down. Then sprinkle the sugar evenly over the butter, and arrange the apple quarters on top in concentric circles.

On a floured surface, roll the puff pastry out to a thickness of ⅛in. Pay attention to the size as you are rolling: it needs to be wide and long enough to cover the apples in the pan. Place the puff pastry gently over the apples, tucking in any excess pastry between the apples and the pan, like a blanket.

Place the pan over medium heat for 5–6 minutes to begin the caramelization process, then put it in the oven for 40 minutes, or until the pastry is golden brown and oozing caramel slightly at the edges.

To make the Calvados Cream, place the crème fraîche, heavy cream, and sugar in a large, clean bowl. Bring them gently together with a spatula until well combined. Add the Calvados and, using a whisk, beat all the ingredients together until you have soft, snowy peaks. Cover and refrigerate until needed.

To serve, turn the tarte tatin onto a cutting board. Cut it in four and place each slice on a plate with a generous spoonful of the cold Calvados Cream.

Serves 4

5 tbsp unsalted butter, softened

⅓ cup superfine sugar

5 Braeburn apples, peeled, cored, and quartered, left in the fridge for at least 3 hours, but preferably overnight

flour, for dusting

4oz puff pastry (ready-made is fine)

For the Calvados cream

⅔ cup crème fraîche

½ cup heavy cream

¼ cup superfine sugar

2 tbsp Calvados

You will need an 8in shallow frying pan with an ovenproof handle.

Bryn's Tips
Leaving apple pieces in the fridge allows them to dry out. Then they won't give off steam when cooking and the pastry will stay crisper. Don't worry if they turn a bit brown—they will be caramelized anyway.

Berries

I gorged myself on berries as a kid. They were everywhere! We picked them from the hedgerows when hunting and as we walked to school. My friend Huw and I would pick strawberries for a local grower for pocket money—cycling to the field in the summer for a session of backbreaking berry picking. No wonder they ask you to pick your own! It's another example of the free food we have access to in the countryside. Like game birds, they're just there. In the fall, we would bring berries home so that Nain and Mam could make jams and chutneys to last us through the cold winter months when everyone craved the sunny, bright flavors of summer. Until then, we'd have oozing crumbles and sticky pies, to be eaten with relish at the kitchen table. That's if there were any berries left by the time we got home... Sometimes temptation would get the better of us, and there'd be none remaining when we reached the front door. But at least we had the excuse that they were packed with vitamin C, and hadn't cost us anything!

Writing this book has made me look again at the way we saw the world as a family—nothing was wasted, and when we came across anything useful, we'd use it. So even if we didn't want all those berries ourselves, they could be made into a preserve, which we could give to someone. And get something back in kind. That's how it used to work. To some extent, it still does.

There are so many types of berry—each with its own unique flavor: raspberries go beautifully with lemon and lemon curd. Puréed or crushed they are wonderful with duck or venison, their acidity cutting through the fattiness. Blackberries and blueberries are good for crumbles, on their own, or mixed with apples. Strawberries with cream, or meringues, and in tarts are gorgeous. Try to find wild strawberries in season for a real treat.

The great thing about berries is that they hold their own so well in both sweet and savory dishes—think of cranberries with roast duck or gooseberries with goose. My rule of thumb is not to have fresh berries on the menu out of season, although I'm happy to use them in confit or preserved. I just think that we should enjoy them in season when they're at their juicy best.

Raspberry Jello

Serves 4–6

2¼lb raspberries (save a few for decoration)

½ cup confectioners' sugar

1 vanilla pod, split in half with the seeds scraped out

3 leaves of gelatin (or half a ¼oz envelope of gelatin)

Jello isn't just for kids' parties. This is a grown-up one—deep, rich red with ripe raspberries and scented with a hint of vanilla. It's great on its own, but I love to ring the changes by serving it with a generous scoop of good ice cream or the Lemon Curd on page 249.

In a large heatproof bowl, mix together the berries, 1 cup water, the confectioners' sugar, and the vanilla pod, including its seeds. Stir them together well, making sure that all the confectioners' sugar has dissolved. Cover the bowl with plastic wrap and set aside.

Bring a large saucepan of water to a boil. Place the covered bowl on top of the saucepan, making sure that the water does not touch the bowl. Turn off the heat and leave the saucepan and bowl as they are for 2–3 hours, until all the raspberry juice has been released.

Set a colander over a clean bowl and line it with a piece of damp muslin. Pour the raspberry mixture into the cloth, and leave to stand for 1 hour, to filter gently through to the bowl. Remove the colander and cloth and pour the liquid into a large measuring cup. You should have about 1 cup, for which you will need 3 leaves of gelatin. Place the gelatin in cold water and set aside to soften.

In a saucepan over medium heat, bring ⅔ cup of the raspberry liquid to a boil. Remove it from the heat, add the softened gelatin to the hot liquid and stir in well. Then pass the liquid through a fine strainer onto the remaining berry juice and mix until combined.

Pour into a decorative mold or individual glasses and, when the jello is cool, put into the fridge to set for at least 3–4 hours or overnight. Top with a few raspberries to serve.

Eton Mess

Serves 4–6

9oz strawberries, hulled and quartered

¼ cup superfine sugar

juice of 1 lemon

⅔ cup heavy cream

7oz meringues, crushed

4½oz raspberries

pinch of vanilla salt (optional; see tip, page 169)

This dessert gets its name from the famous boys' school in England, where they have been serving it since the 1930s. I love the simplicity—just fruit, cream, and meringue—it's so summery and fresh. I like to add a pinch of vanilla salt at the end, for an extra kick of flavor. Serve this dessert in individual glasses so you can see the layers.

In a large bowl, mix the strawberries, sugar, and lemon juice together. Set aside.

In another bowl, whip the heavy cream to soft peaks. Add the crushed meringues and mix in gently, but well. Set aside.

Roughly crush the raspberries with a fork and set aside.

Now spoon the raspberries evenly into individual glasses. Cover with the cream and meringue mixture, then pour the strawberries and their juice over the top. Add the vanilla salt and refrigerate until you are ready to serve.

Berries

Strawberry Jam Doughnuts

Hot, fluffy doughnuts oozing fresh homemade strawberry jam and dusted with sugar that sticks to your chops... yum! If you don't have a deep-fat fryer, I'm sorry, but I really wouldn't attempt these. Feel free to substitute a different jam, though. I just love strawberry. Note that I'm using fresh yeast here. If you can't get it (although it is available from bakeries), use compressed yeast (found in the dairy section of supermarkets) or active dry or instant yeast. Follow the conversion formula on the package.

First, make the strawberry jam. In a heavy-bottomed pan, bring the strawberry purée and the sugar to a boil over low heat and simmer for 6–7 minutes, until the mixture is thick enough to coat the back of a spoon. Take off the heat and set aside to cool. Then stir in the lime juice.

Now for the doughnuts. Put the flour and the sugar into an electric mixer fitted with a dough hook.

Dissolve the yeast thoroughly in the lukewarm milk. Then, with the mixer going, pour the yeasted milk mixture onto the flour and sugar and mix together. Add the egg and the softened butter, and combine until the dough is smooth and shiny. If the dough feels too wet to handle, add another spoonful of flour to bring it together. Cover the bowl with a damp cloth and leave the dough to rise in a warm place for about 1 hour.

Punch down the dough with your fist. Turn the dough onto a well-floured surface and knead it for a good 5 minutes. It should become shiny and smooth, silky and elastic.

Divide the dough into 10–12 small pieces. Roll each into a ball. Place the balls, spaced apart, on a well-oiled baking sheet and leave in a warm place until they have doubled in size.

Set the deep-fat fryer to 356°F. Fry the doughnuts until golden all over. Remove from the fryer and place on paper towels to drain.

Pour the strawberry jam into a piping bag with a nozzle or a plastic squeeze bottle with a nozzle. Jab the doughnuts with the nozzle and pipe in the jam. Then roll them in the vanilla sugar to finish, and serve warm.

Makes 10–12

For the strawberry jam

12oz strawberries, hulled and puréed

½ cup superfine sugar

juice of ½ lime

For the doughnuts

1⅔ cups white flour, plus extra for dusting

2 tbsp superfine sugar

¼oz fresh yeast

7 tbsp lukewarm milk

1 egg

¼ cup butter, softened

vegetable oil, for deep-frying

½ cup vanilla sugar (see page 216)

You will need a deep-fat fryer.

Mixed Berry Clafoutis

A delicious combination of creamy, custardy batter and tart fruit, this is a classic and makes an indulgent end to any meal. You could make it with literally any fruit you want: figs, gooseberries, slightly precooked apples—all these are delicious and ensure that this is not just a summer dessert.

Preheat the oven to 325°F.

Sift the flour into a large bowl. Add the sugar and stir. Pour in the cream, followed by the eggs, and stir together well. Finish the batter by adding the melted butter, again stirring well to combine all the ingredients.

Scatter the fruit evenly over the base of the prepared cake pan or individual tart pans. Pour the batter evenly over the fruit.

In the cake pan, bake the clafoutis for 30 minutes, until golden. For individual servings, bake for 8–12 minutes until golden. Serve warm.

Serves 4

½ cup all-purpose flour

¼ cup superfine sugar

½ cup heavy cream

2 eggs

3 tbsp butter, melted and cooled

4oz blueberries

4oz red currants

4oz cherries, pitted and cut in half

You will need an 8in cake pan or individual tart pans, greased with butter

Blackberry Soufflé

Serves 8

For the molds

¼ cup unsalted butter, softened

¼ cup superfine sugar

For the soufflé

1¼lb blackberries, puréed and strained to remove the seeds

2 tbsp cornstarch

¾ cup superfine sugar

9 egg whites

confectioners' sugar, for dusting

So many people worry about making a soufflé, but it's really not that hard. This one makes a light, fluffy dessert with the delicious tartness of blackberries. And the real plus is that it can be made in advance. You can prepare the jam at least the day before, while the soufflé is happy to sit for up to three hours before going into the oven.

Preheat the oven to 350°F.

Take six soufflé dishes or ramekins, and brush the insides with the softened butter. Then dust them with the superfine sugar and set aside in the refrigerator until needed.

Bring the blackberry purée to a boil in a heavy-bottomed saucepan over low heat, and simmer for 2 minutes.

In a small bowl, dissolve the cornstarch in 2 tbsp water and pour it into the purée. Stir well. Now add ½ cup of the sugar and simmer until you have reduced the purée to a jamlike consistency. Keep whisking the mixture every 1–2 minutes to prevent it from sticking or burning. You should now have 9–10oz of jam. Set it aside to cool.

In a clean, dry bowl, add the remaining superfine sugar to the egg whites and whisk them into soft peaks. Take one spoonful of the whites and whisk it into the jam, just to loosen the mixture. Then gently fold in the rest of the egg whites, until well combined.

Divide the mixture between the six dishes or ramekins and place them in the oven for 9–11 minutes. When the soufflés have risen, dust the tops with confectioners' sugar and place each one on a large plate. Serve with a scoop of vanilla ice cream.

Bryn's Tips
To make these in advance, beat the egg whites into the jam, as above, then put them in the fridge for up to 3 hours before you need to cook them. Bake as above and serve immediately.

Chocolate

When I was a kid, chocolate was special. Not rationed, exactly, but not something I could have all the time, either. On trips into town, I'd be allowed to go into the store to choose one treat. It would always be chocolate. I think this has influenced me more than I know, because as soon as I became a chef, I took every opportunity to use chocolate whenever and wherever I wanted. And I knew that when I was writing the list of ingredients for this book, there was no way I could leave it out.

It's not just the flavor; there's something romantic about chocolate. It's another of those sexy ingredients—smooth and silky on the tongue, sensuous in the pan when you stir it, and just by looking at it you know it will bring good times. It literally melts in the mouth: its melting point is just below body temperature! Chocolate is guaranteed to lighten people's hearts and make them smile. There are customers at the restaurant whose eyes swing straight to the dessert menu looking for a chocolate delight, and they plan the rest of their order just to save room for it.

As a chef, I know a certain amount about chocolate, but the people who make chocolate are amazing, from those who grow the cacao, harvest, and dry it, to those who refine it and temper it to glossy perfection. It really is an art form, a passion. And what a journey to get to our plates!

As ever in cooking, the quality of the ingredient is of utmost importance. Today, we have a very wide choice in chocolate, and there are many wonderful products available. Some are sourced from specific estates or *terroir,* some are made from a single variety of cocoa bean, and some contain up to 90 percent cocoa solids. I tend to recommend those with 70 percent cocoa solids in most of the recipes in this chapter—plenty of chocolatey bang for your buck. But in the Chocolate Whiskey Truffles on page 199, I suggest that you use a 64 percent chocolate, as a higher percentage might mask the glorious whiskey flavor. Similarly, with the Chocolate Orange Molten cake on page 205, I order a special orange flavored chocolate from my friend, Toby Beevers at Kokonoir Chocolate. It's a fantastic product, although in the recipe here I'm using orange zest to make things easier.

But remember: quality is not measured in cocoa solids alone; the other ingredients in the chocolate bar matter, too. The bottom line, when shopping for all ingredients, is to get the best you can afford and the taste you prefer.

Chocolate Whiskey Truffles

Ever since Penderyn Welsh whiskey was launched in 2004, I've wanted to marry it with something rich and chocolatey. These truffles are the perfect solution. Feel free to use any whiskey you like—or to substitute brandy or rum if you prefer.

Place the chocolate pieces in a heatproof bowl. In a heavy-bottomed saucepan bring the cream to a boil. Remove from the heat immediately and pour over the chocolate. Stir well until the chocolate is completely melted.

Whisk in the whiskey until well combined, then put the bowl into the refrigerator for 4 hours.

Using a melon-baller or a teaspoon, scoop the chocolate into balls, then roll them in the cocoa. Refrigerate for at least 1 hour before serving.

BRYN'S TIPS
I find 64 percent cocoa solids work best for this. You can use 70 percent or richer if you prefer, but "heavier" chocolate fights against the whiskey.

Makes about 36

9oz good-quality dark chocolate, minimum 64 percent cocoa solids, broken into very small pieces—each no bigger than ½in

⅓ cup heavy cream

¼ cup whiskey

2 tbsp cocoa powder, for coating

Chocolate Sponge Cake

Serves 8–10

3 eggs

7 tbsp superfine sugar

½ cup all-purpose flour

5 tbsp cocoa powder

1 tsp baking powder

4–6 tbsp cherry jam

1 cup cream, whipped

You will need an 8in round cake pan, lined with parchment paper.

This is a really good chocolate cake, and a favorite in our household. I serve it here with jam and cream, but you could cover it in a chocolate icing or ganache, or simply sprinkle it with cocoa powder and confectioners' sugar.

Preheat the oven to 325°F.

In a large bowl, beat the eggs and sugar together until they double in size. Sift the flour, cocoa, and baking powder together, then very gently fold them into the egg and sugar mixture, making sure that you keep the mixture as light and airy as possible. This is the way to produce a light and airy sponge.

Pour the mixture into the lined cake pan and bake for 20–25 minutes. Do not open the oven door until you think it is ready—the cake may collapse! To check whether the cake is cooked, stab it gently in the middle with a toothpick. If the stick comes out clean, the cake is done; if not, give it a few more minutes in the oven.

When the cake is ready, remove it from the oven. Leave it in the pan for about 10 minutes, then turn it onto a wire rack to cool completely.

To serve, slice the cake in two through the center and fill with some cherry jam and whipped cream before reassembling.

Chocolate Brownies

Who doesn't love a gooey, sticky, chocolatey brownie, still warm from the oven? They brighten up any snacktime, and are terrific as a dessert with a scoop of good ice cream. Feel free to add some nuts if you like—about 3½oz will do the trick.

Preheat the oven to 325°F.

Place the chocolate and the butter in a heatproof bowl over a saucepan of barely simmering water, making sure that the bowl does not touch the water. Stir the chocolate and butter together, until melted and well combined. Set aside to cool.

In a separate bowl, whisk the eggs and sugar together until light and creamy. Pour the cooled melted chocolate mixture into the sugar and eggs, and then gently fold in the flour. (If you want to add nuts, gently stir them in now.)

Pour the mixture into the lined baking pan and bake for 25–35 minutes, or until the brownies have a slightly crackled appearance on the surface. Remove from the oven and leave to cool in the pan before cutting into squares.

Makes 12

9oz good-quality dark chocolate, minimum 70 percent cocoa solids

1¾ cups butter

5 eggs

2 cups superfine sugar

pinch of salt

1½ cups all-purpose flour

You will need a 10 × 12in brownie pan, lined with parchment paper.

Chocolate Chestnut Cake with Confit Cranberries

Serves 8

For the chocolate sponge

2 cups milk

18oz cooked chestnuts, chopped

3½oz good-quality dark chocolate, minimum 70 percent cocoa solids

½ cup unsalted butter

4 eggs

½ cup superfine sugar

¾ cup ground almonds

2 tsp cornstarch

zest of 1 orange

For the confit cranberries

⅔ cup simple syrup (see page 175)

2oz cooked chestnuts, left whole

2oz pistachio nuts

2oz cranberries

juice of 1 orange

You will need an 8in loose-bottomed cake pan, buttered.

I love the way in which the nutty chocolate works against the tartness of the cranberries in this rich and decadent dessert. It makes a great finish to a meal during the festive season.

Preheat the oven 325°F.

To make the chocolate sponge, place the milk and the chopped chestnuts in a heavy-bottomed saucepan over medium heat. Bring the milk to a boil and simmer for 20 minutes. Remove from the heat and let it cool a little. Carefully pour into a blender or food processor and blend to a smooth purée. Pour into a clean bowl and set aside.

Place the chocolate and the butter in a heatproof bowl over a saucepan of barely simmering water, making sure that the bowl does not touch the water, and stir until all the butter and chocolate have melted. Set aside and keep warm.

Using a food processor, or by hand, beat the eggs and the sugar together, until thick and creamy.

Mix the ground almonds, the cornstarch, and the orange zest together.

Gently fold the chocolate mixture into the chestnut purée, then, just as gently, fold in the beaten eggs, followed by the dry ingredients. Transfer the mixture into the buttered cake pan and bake for 40 minutes, or until the top of the cake is firm to the touch. If you stab the cake with a toothpick, the toothpick should come out clean.

While the cake is cooking, make the confit cranberries. Bring the simple syrup to a simmer, add the chestnuts, pistachio nuts, cranberries, and orange juice and cook for about 40 minutes, or until just soft. Set aside to cool.

When the cake is ready, remove from the oven and let it rest in the pan for 10 minutes before turning it onto a wire rack to cool. Serve in slices with a spoonful of confit cranberries on the top.

Chocolate Orange Molten Cake, Yogurt Ice Cream, & Candied Peel

Molten cake is a benchmark of a chef's skill, and this combination of chocolate and orange is amazing. I recommend that you make the ice cream and candied peel the day before. If you don't have an ice-cream maker, serve with a helping of fresh yogurt instead.

First, make the ice cream. Beat the egg yolks and the sugar in a bowl until thick and creamy. Set aside. Pour the milk and cream into a heavy-bottomed saucepan and bring to a boil over low heat. Now pour the hot milk onto the egg-yolk mixture and stir well. Return the mixture to a clean saucepan and stir, over low heat, until the mixture thickens enough to coat the back of a spoon. Pass the mixture through a fine strainer onto the yogurt, and stir well to mix thoroughly. Let it cool, then chill in the fridge. Pour the chilled mixture into the ice-cream maker and churn until frozen, but not too stiff. Put into a container and freeze until needed.

To make the candied peel, thoroughly wash the orange, then peel it as thinly as you can, making sure there is no bitter pith attached to the skin. Using a sharp knife, cut the peel into very fine strips. Blanch the peel in boiling water for 1 minute. Drain and refresh in a bowl of cold water. Repeat the blanching and refreshing process twice more.

In a heavy-bottomed pan, bring ⅓ cup water, the sugar, and star anise to a boil slowly, making sure that the sugar dissolves completely. Add the blanched orange peel and simmer over low heat for 1 hour. Take it off the heat and let it cool slightly. Using a fork, remove the peel from the syrup and roll it in the extra superfine sugar. Place on a wire rack to cool. Store the candied peel in an airtight container until needed.

Butter the molds and dust them with cocoa, shaking out any excess. Put in the fridge.

Put the chocolate, butter, and orange zest in a heatproof bowl over a saucepan of barely simmering water, and stir occasionally until the chocolate and butter have melted. Set the bowl aside to cool a little. Beat the eggs, egg yolks, and sugar in a large bowl thoroughly but gently—don't add too many air bubbles. Pour the chocolate mixture into the egg mixture and stir well to combine, then gently fold in the flour. Tap the bowl on the table to help remove any air bubbles from the mixture. Pour carefully into the molds, until each is about half full. Put in the fridge for at least 30 minutes, or overnight.

When you are ready to cook the molten cakes, preheat the oven to 325°F. Bake the molten cakes in the oven for 15 minutes. Set aside, in the molds, for 2 minutes. To serve, turn the molten cakes onto a plate, arrange a scoop of the ice cream (or plain yogurt) on the side, and scatter candied peel over the top.

Serves 6

For the yogurt ice cream

2 egg yolks

⅓ cup superfine sugar

¾ cup whole milk

¼ cup heavy cream

18oz plain yogurt

For the candied orange peel

1 large orange

½ cup superfine sugar, plus 2–3 tbsp for rolling

1 star anise

For the molten cakes

1 cup unsalted butter, plus extra for greasing

cocoa powder, for dusting

9oz good-quality dark chocolate, minimum 70 percent cocoa solids

1 tsp grated orange zest

5 eggs, plus 5 egg yolks

⅔ cup superfine sugar

2 tsp all-purpose flour

You will need six ovenproof molds, each about 3in in diameter.

Cream

There is no way I could leave a dairy product out of this book—and what better choice for inclusion than the king of dairy, cream? In our house, we boys would fight over the two inches of cream sitting at the top of the old-fashioned glass milk bottles. Just hearing the clanking of the bottles on the doorstep was enough to get us out of our beds and rushing downstairs. Which reminds me: where has the "top of the milk" gone? You just don't find it in the plastic cartons you buy at the supermarket. It's all a far cry from the dairy on my uncle's farm, which contained more cream than you could dream of.

To this day, I can close my eyes and walk through the farmyard into the white-washed dairy building with its huge red sliding doors. Open those doors, and you stepped into a different world: spotless, sparkling, and sterile-clean. Massive metal and glass pipes ran overhead, milk gushing through them—like something out of Willy Wonka's chocolate factory—and sploshing into big silver churns, everything constantly moving. It was a magical place for a boy, and it gave us the creamiest, purest milk I've ever tasted.

There was always a big pitcher of this milk in the kitchen at home, fresh and warm, frothy on the top like a giant cappuccino, and full of fatty yellow cream. We'd walk from home down to the yard to get it, straight from the churn. Of course, all the milking was done by machine, but occasionally I'd try by hand myself. It would be hard work to milk a whole herd by hand, I can tell you! But if you've never milked a cow and you get the chance, do give it a try. It's a reminder, once again, not just of where our food comes from, but of our connection to the land, the farms, and the animals that sustain us.

Cream is a remarkable ingredient, not least for its versatility. It's not just for sweet dishes, but savory ones, too—a spoonful or two enriches sauces and adds a silkiness to soups, providing an easy route to a little luxury. And I always use heavy cream in my cooking—I think it is the real deal, or nothing!

Lemon Posset, Strawberries, & Basil

Serves 4

For the posset

juice and zest of 2 lemons

1⅔ cups heavy cream

⅔ cup superfine sugar

For the strawberries

14–18oz strawberries

1 tbsp sugar

handful of baby basil leaves, or larger basil leaves torn at the last minute

Who couldn't fall in love with this wonderfully sharp and refreshing yet decadent treat? It's a dream of a dessert. I love to see chemistry in action as the acid in the lemon works its magic to set the cream. I serve this with the Shortbread on page 225, for added crunch. If you don't want to add the strawberries, a plain posset is fantastic, too.

Put the lemon juice in a heatproof bowl and set aside.

Bring the heavy cream, the sugar, and the lemon zest to a boil in a heavy-bottomed saucepan over medium heat. As soon as it reaches a boil, remove from the heat.

Pour the simmering cream onto the lemon juice—you must do it this way around: if you add the lemon juice to the hot cream, it will curdle. Watch the cream begin to thicken as it hits the lemon juice, then pass the mixture through a fine strainer into a clean bowl.

Divide the posset equally between four heatproof glasses or ramekins, and set aside to cool. Then place in the refrigerator for at least 2 hours, or until set.

To prepare the strawberries, hull and quarter them, and place in a bowl. Sprinkle with the sugar and leave to sit for about 40 minutes, until they release their juices, then add the basil leaves.

To serve, divide the strawberries equally and place them on top of each lemon posset. Pour the strawberry juice over the top and serve cold.

BRYN'S TIPS
You can make this dessert the day before serving; just keep it covered in the fridge.

Bara Brith & Butter Pudding

A Welsh take on classic bread and butter pudding, this recipe uses the traditional bara brith or speckled bread I grew up with. My Nain's recipe on page 237 is simply fantastic.

Serves 6–8

1 whole Nain's Bara Brith (see page 237)

¼ cup unsalted butter, softened

6 eggs

½ cup superfine sugar

1 quart milk

1 vanilla pod, split in half with the seeds scraped out

3 tbsp dark brown sugar

Preheat the oven to 300°F.

Cut the bara brith into ½in slices, trimming off the crusts, then cut each slice into triangles. Spread the slices with the softened butter, then neatly arrange the bara brith in a buttered serving dish. You can overlap the slices so that they all fit in.

In a large, heatproof bowl, beat the eggs and the sugar together until light and creamy.

Bring the milk and the vanilla pod and seeds to a boil in a saucepan, take off the heat immediately, then pour onto the eggs and sugar, whisking all the time until the mixture thickens into a custard.

Pass the custard through a fine strainer onto the bara brith slices. Sprinkle the surface evenly with the brown sugar.

Place the dish in a roasting pan half filled with warm water and cook in the oven for 40–50 minutes. Serve hot.

Buttermilk Pannacotta with Poached Rhubarb & Ginger

Serves 4

3 leaves of gelatin (or half a ¼oz envelope of gelatin)

¾ cup heavy cream

½ cup superfine sugar

1 vanilla pod, split in half with the seeds scraped out

¾ cup buttermilk

⅔ cup ginger wine

½ cup light brown sugar

strip of orange zest

9oz rhubarb, trimmed and cut into 1in sticks

I always seem to have a pannacotta on the menu. I just love them—they're simple to make and a great foil both to compotes and fresh fruit. The buttermilk lightens this recipe, and gives it a lovely tangy quality.

If using leaf gelatin, soak the gelatin leaves in cold water until soft. Set aside.

In a large, heavy-bottomed saucepan, bring the heavy cream, superfine sugar, and vanilla pod and seeds to a boil. As soon as everything boils, remove the pan from the heat. You can scoop out the vanilla pod, too.

Add the softened gelatin to the hot liquid and stir well until dissolved. Pour the liquid onto the cold buttermilk and whisk together until combined. Pass the mixture through a fine strainer, then pour into four heatproof glasses or ramekins. Place in the refrigerator to set. This should take about 2 hours.

While the pannacotta is setting, gently heat the ginger wine with the light brown sugar and the orange zest in a large, shallow pan until the sugar has dissolved. Add the rhubarb sticks and poach gently for 4–6 minutes, or until just soft. Remove from the heat, leaving the rhubarb to cool in the liquid.

To serve, spoon the rhubarb on top of each chilled pannacotta, and drizzle the rhubarb and ginger sauce over the top.

Cream

Crème Brûlée

Cracking through the caramel on top of one of these beauties into the creamy vanilla center has to be one of life's great pleasures. It's pure dinner theater!

Preheat the oven to 250°F.

In a large bowl, whisk the egg yolks with ⅓ cup of the sugar, until pale and thick. Set aside.

In a heavy-bottomed saucepan, bring the cream, the milk, and the vanilla seeds to a boil. Immediately take the pan off the heat, and pour the boiling cream onto the sugar and egg mixture. Stir well to combine. Then pass the custard through a fine strainer and pour into individual ramekins.

Place the ramekins in a roasting pan, then pour warm water into the pan so that it reaches halfway up the sides of the ramekins. This will help the brûlées to cook evenly. Bake in the oven for 30–40 minutes, then remove and set aside to cool.

When the brûlées are completely cold, sprinkle with the remaining sugar and caramelize with a blow torch or under the broiler. Serve when the caramel is cold and crunchy.

Serves 6–8

7 egg yolks

⅔ cup superfine sugar

1 cup plus 2 tbsp heavy cream

⅔ cup milk

1 vanilla pod, split in half with the seeds scraped out—you only need the seeds

Rice Pudding

Serves 6

⅔ cup heavy cream

1 cup milk

1 vanilla pod, split in half with the seeds scraped out

½ cup risotto rice

4 egg yolks

⅓ cup superfine sugar

3 tbsp heavy cream, whipped into soft peaks

As kids, we ate rice pudding regularly because we had the best milk and cream at our fingertips, courtesy of my uncle's lovely cows. I've made this one a little richer than usual, adding extra cream, and I serve it chilled. It's delicious with a scoop of the Lemon Curd on page 249 or with some fresh, seasonal fruit.

In a heavy-bottomed saucepan, bring the heavy cream, the milk, and the vanilla pod to a boil. Add the rice and continue to cook at a rolling boil until the rice is soft, stirring occasionally to stop it from sticking to the bottom of the pan. This should take 10–12 minutes.

By the time the rice is cooked, the cream and milk should be thick and coating the rice. Remove the pan from the heat and set aside to cool.

In a large bowl, whisk the egg yolks and the sugar together until creamy, then add them to the rice. Ensure that the rice is warm rather than hot—if it is too hot, the eggs will scramble.

Stir well to combine, then place the saucepan back over very low heat, stirring the rice pudding constantly for 2–3 minutes, until the mixture has thickened and the egg yolks are cooked. When it is done, the mixture should coat the back of a spoon.

Now pour the rice pudding into a large baking pan to cool—you need to stop it from cooking as quickly as possible, and the extra surface area helps. Once the pudding is cool, cover it with plastic wrap and place it in the refrigerator until completely cold.

Transfer the rice pudding to a clean bowl. Gently fold in the whipped cream to lighten the mixture. To serve, spoon the pudding into individual bowls or glasses.

BRYN'S TIPS
Do save the scraped vanilla pod. Tuck it into a jar of sugar to make vanilla sugar for baking. Keep adding sugar to the jar as you use it.

Baked Goods

It's the smell, really, isn't it? If I close my eyes, it takes me back to my Mam's kitchen, when there was always something in the oven, be it scones for tea, a jelly roll that would be served oozing with homemade strawberry jam, or some cookies to take to school. The smell reminds me that there is something very special about baking for someone. It's a personal act—a very loving act.

Teatimes on the farm were not the sit-down affair people often think of. They weren't posh. Unless, of course, we had friends coming over or it was a special occasion—then we'd have to dress up and sit in the parlor. No, for me, teatime was synonymous with work on the farm. Usually, we'd have something freshly baked, eaten on a seat on the back of a tractor and washed down with a flask of sweet tea, in a field far away from the farmhouse. We needed that stop-gap between lunch and dinner to keep our strength up. It was refueling. It's the same for me now. I always have a cup of tea and something sweet around 4 o'clock. The tradition continues—even if I'm not in that field anymore!

Cakes are very versatile, though. They're not just for tea or midmorning breaks. You can slice a plain cake, serve it on a pretty plate, spruced up with a scoop of good ice cream or a fruity sauce, and voilà!—a great homemade dessert. Add some nuts to the basic cake mixture—their oils will give the cake a really moist texture and help it keep longer, too. Even leftover crumbs can be mixed with some dried fruit and used to fill an Eccles cake. But that's not the only reason I like to have a cake on the menu. People love it. A good cake is a strange combination of indulgent richness and the comforts of home. You can't go wrong with that.

As always when baking, use the best ingredients you can afford. Great butter, great eggs, and the right flour make a real difference to the end product. Take your time, too. Prepare and measure your ingredients and follow the recipe—this is where chemistry and cooking go hand in hand. Get the temperature right. Make sure your pan, if you are using one, is the right size. I like loose-bottomed pans, since they make removing the cake from the pan nice and easy. Remember, once the cake is in that oven, there's no turning back!

So go on—bake yourself and your loved ones a sweet treat. You know they're worth it.

Jelly Roll

I remember making this in cooking class at school. I loved rolling the cake up around all that oozing jam. You can use fillings other than jam—the Lemon Curd on page 249 makes a fantastic alternative or I sometimes use sweetened cream cheese when serving this as a dessert.

Preheat the oven to 350°F.

Beat the eggs and sugar together in a large bowl—using a hand whisk or an electric mixer—until the mixture is light and creamy and has doubled in size.

Fold in the flour very gently so that you do not lose any of the airy volume that makes this cake so light.

Pour the mixture carefully onto the lined baking sheet and cook in the oven for 6 minutes, or until pale golden brown.

While the cake is in the oven, gently warm the jam in a small saucepan and set aside.

Lay a clean dish towel on the work surface and sprinkle with 1 tablespoon superfine sugar. Turn the cake onto the sugared cloth and gently peel away the paper. Spread the surface of the cake generously with the warm jam, then, using the cloth, roll the cake away from you, up into a fairly tight roll. Leave the cloth in place on the outside of the roll for a few minutes. Then remove the cloth and gently transfer the jelly roll to a wire rack to cool.

Makes 8–10 slices

3 eggs

⅓ cup superfine sugar, plus 1 tbsp for sprinkling

⅔ cup all-purpose flour

3½oz raspberry jam

You will need a 15 × 12in baking sheet, lined with parchment paper.

Spice Cake

Serves 8

½ cup milk

½ cup golden syrup (or honey)

1 tsp baking soda

½ cup superfine sugar

10 tbsp butter, softened

1 egg

2¼ cups all-purpose flour

1 tsp ground cinnamon

1 tsp ground ginger

⅔ cup dark brown sugar

You will need a 1lb
loaf pan, lined with
parchment paper.

As with the sticky gingerbread of my childhood, I like to eat thick slices of this cake buttered for a late breakfast. At the restaurant we toast it, then make it into crumbs to use as a base for cheesecakes or to sprinkle onto ice cream.

Preheat the oven to 325°F.

Bring the milk and golden syrup to a simmer in a saucepan over low heat. Remove from the heat, add the baking soda and set aside.

In a large bowl, or using a food processor, cream the sugar and the butter together until pale and fluffy, then add the egg, beating well.

Sift the flour, cinnamon, and ginger together and gently fold them into the creamed butter. Now pour in the warm milk, making sure everything is well combined.

Pour the mixture into the pan and bake for 40 minutes. When it is done, leave it in the pan for about 10 minutes, then turn onto a wire rack to cool completely.

Shortbread

I can't think back to my childhood without remembering crisp, buttery shortbread cookies, shared at the kitchen table with big glasses of fresh milk. I still love them like that. But I also like to serve them with strawberries and cream, or on the side of a Lemon Posset (see page 210), where they set a lovely sweet crunch against the dessert's tart creaminess.

Sift the flour and salt into a bowl. Make a well in the middle of the flour with your hands. Place the butter and sugar in the center of the well and, using your fingertips, start to bring the flour into the well, rubbing it into the butter and sugar until all the flour has been incorporated.

Add the egg yolk. Then, using your hands again, bring the dough together into a ball, wrap it in plastic wrap, and place in the refrigerator for 2 hours.

Preheat the oven to 350°F.

On a well-floured surface, roll out the dough to a thickness of ¼in. Then, with a sharp knife, cut it into fingers, each about 1in wide and 3in long.

Place the fingers on the prepared baking sheet, sprinkle with a little extra sugar, and bake for 12–15 minutes, or until a pale golden color. Remove from the oven and leave to cool a little on the baking sheet before transferring the fingers to a wire rack to cool completely.

Makes 12–14 good-sized bars

2 cups all-purpose flour, plus extra for dusting

pinch of salt

1 cup butter, softened

½ cup superfine sugar, plus extra for sprinkling

1 egg yolk

You will need a baking sheet lined with parchment paper.

Pistachio Cake

Serves 6

⅔ cup ground almonds

3½oz pistachio nuts

9 tbsp butter

⅔ cup superfine sugar

¾oz pistachio paste
(see tip, below)

3 eggs

confectioners' sugar, for
dusting

You will need an 11 × 8in
baking sheet lined with
parchment paper.

I wanted to put a cake on the dessert menu and so, after playing
around with different ideas and ingredients, I came up with
this stunning, pale-jade winner. I like to serve it with a pitcher
of cold custard on the side, or a scoop of the Apple Sorbet
on page 175.

Preheat the oven to 325°F.

Put the ground almonds and the pistachio nuts into a blender or food processor and chop
or grind them until very finely ground. Set aside.

In a large, clean bowl, cream together the butter and superfine sugar until pale, light, and
fluffy. Add the pistachio paste and the finely ground nuts, mixing them in gently until
smooth. Add the eggs one by one, beating well after each addition, then pour the batter
into the lined baking sheet. Use a spoon or spatula to smooth out the batter evenly.

Bake for 30 minutes, or until golden brown and firm to the touch. The cake should spring
back when you press it gently with your finger. Then remove the cake from the oven and
allow it to cool in the tray.

When the cake is cool, cut it into square tiles, and serve dusted with confectioners'
sugar. The cake will stay moist for 2–3 days because of the oil from the nuts.

BRYN'S TIPS
*You can buy pistachio paste in specialty baking stores or online, but if you cannot find it, substitute
an extra ounce of ground pistachio nuts.*

Madeleines

These gorgeous little shell-shaped treats are sure to impress. The smell when they are baking is one of the loveliest in cooking—a gentle, citrusy, almost honeyed scent. Irresistible!

In a large bowl, gently beat the eggs with the superfine sugar, until light and creamy. Add the lemon and orange zest. Sift the flour and baking powder together, and gently fold them into the mixture. Then fold in the ground almonds followed by the melted butter. Do not overwork or overbeat the mixture. It should be light and airy, so treat it kindly. Set aside to rest for 1 hour.

Preheat the oven to 350°F.

Using a spoon or a piping bag, fill each mold in the madeleine pan to three-quarters of its volume—the mixture will rise in the oven.

If you're making smaller, petit-four-sized madeleines, bake them in the oven for 5–6 minutes. If you're making larger ones, bake them for 10–12 minutes. In both cases, be careful not to overcook the madeleines: they should stay moist, smell delicious, and have a lovely golden color.

As soon as they are cooked, turn the madeleines out of the molds onto a wire rack to cool. They are best served warm with a light dusting of confectioners' sugar.

Makes 30–40 petit-four-sized cakes, or 12–16 larger ones

2 eggs

½ cup superfine sugar

zest of 1 lemon

zest of 1 orange

½ cup flour

1 tsp baking powder

⅓ cup ground almonds

5 tbsp butter, melted

confectioners' sugar, for dusting

You will need a madeleine pan, greased and floured.

BRYN'S TIPS
Madeleine pans are available in cookware stores or online. The shallow tray has small, shell-shaped indentations into which you spoon or pipe the batter.

Bread

Bread is where it all began for me. We went on a school trip to the bakery. I vividly remember walking through the village, holding hands with my school-friend Ffion—we can't even have been 10 years old. We watched master baker Alwyn Thomas making dough and baking loaves. We even got to try it ourselves. It seemed magical: here was a man who took dusty flour and, with water, yeast, and heat, made something delicious. I was hooked.

My first job was in that bakery, working Saturday mornings 9–11, for the equivalent of a dollar an hour. I loved it. And by the time I was 14, I'd begun to work there every Saturday, starting at 4am and finishing at noon. I was obsessed; I'd even deliver my bread to the stores to ensure the loaves were displayed just right. After all, I'd made that bread. I'd kneaded it, proofed it, and nursed it, and I wanted it to look beautiful on the shelf.

Alwyn Thomas is the reason I became a chef. It's no exaggeration to say that the bakery shaped everything I've done since. It fired my passion for cooking and gave me a creative outlet for the work ethic I inherited from my Dad. "If you want something," he always told me, "work hard and you'll get it." The bakery proved him right.

Bread is still a key part of my day. Baking it is one of the first jobs each morning at the restaurant. It tastes incredible right out of the oven, and makes the restaurant smell fantastic. It's good for the soul, too. Just kneading dough seems to reconnect us with something primal and important, perhaps because yeast is a living thing. It's delicate and vulnerable, and needs to be nurtured. Hot water will kill it; cold water will put it to sleep. But when the temperature of the liquid is right—about body heat—you can feel the dough come alive in your hands, becoming silky and sexy to the touch. It smells of life itself. Nothing in cooking beats that. This is why I encourage you to use fresh yeast in these recipes. But if you can't find it, feel free to substitute active dry or instant yeast instead. Just follow the instructions on the package. If you make too much bread, it freezes beautifully. Just be sure that you freeze it as soon as you can after it has cooled down. You can make bread crumbs and freeze them, too.

Be confident when you are baking bread. Don't feel as if you are a slave to the dough! If there are two stages of proofing to be done, don't worry too much about the first one—after all, you are going to punch it back down again. It's the second proofing, the one just before it goes in the oven, that is the more important one. That's the one to be precise with, or your bread may come out a little too dense in texture. Play around with shapes and sizes. Scatter some seeds or sea salt on top of a loaf. Learn to feel that sense of being at one with the dough. You'll be a convert to the bread-making cause before you know it!

Bread Sticks

Makes about 16 sticks

¼oz fresh yeast

⅔ cup lukewarm water

1 cup white bread flour, plus extra for dusting

1 tsp salt

These are simple to make at home, and add retro fun to the table. I regard them as an introduction to bread-making—for kids or adults. They teach the touch and feel of dough, and there's no waiting around for anything to proof or rise. I often serve them with the Mackerel Pâté on page 106.

Preheat the oven to 350°F.

Grease a large baking sheet. Dissolve the yeast thoroughly in the lukewarm water. Then put the flour and salt in a bowl and pour in the yeast-infused water.

Mix the flour and water together well until you have a cohesive mass, and everything holds together well—it should not be sticky or gluelike!

Turn the dough out onto a floured surface and knead for about 5 minutes, until the dough is stretchy and feels silky.

Divide the dough into about 16 pieces, then roll out each one with your hands until it is about 12in long.

Place the bread sticks onto the baking sheet, dust with a little flour, cover, and leave to rest for 5 minutes.

Put the tray in the oven and bake the bread sticks for 4–6 minutes, until golden brown. Remove from the tray and place on a wire rack to cool.

Bryn's Tips
For an easy antipasto platter, take the slightly warm bread sticks, dip them in mayonnaise, then roll them in poppy or sesame seeds, and serve with cold cuts or smoked salmon.

Focaccia

Thanks to its olive oil, this traditional Italian bread has a wonderfully airy yet chewy texture. I've added sundried tomatoes to this loaf, but you could leave it plain or add some black olives, rosemary, or even different colored roasted peppers.

Makes 1 loaf

½oz fresh yeast

⅔ cup lukewarm water

3 cups white bread flour, plus extra for dusting

1 tsp sugar

3 tsp sea salt

2 tbsp olive oil

a bunch of basil

3½oz sundried tomatoes

You will need a 12 × 8in baking sheet lined with parchment paper.

Dissolve the yeast thoroughly in the lukewarm water. Mix the flour, sugar, and 2 teaspoons of the sea salt together in a large bowl with the olive oil, and make a well in the center with your hands. Then pour in the yeast-infused water.

Using your fingertips, bring the flour into the water to make a cohesive dough. Gather it up, then knead it gently on a floured surface for 3–4 minutes, until the dough is smooth and elastic.

Place the dough in a clean bowl, cover with a damp dish towel, and leave to rise for 30–40 minutes.

When the dough has doubled in size, transfer it to a floured surface and roll it out to a thickness of 1in. Place it on the lined baking sheet. With a pair of sharp scissors, make several cuts in the dough and place 1 basil leaf and 1 sundried tomato in each cut. Repeat until the surface is evenly covered with basil and tomatoes, and then sprinkle with the remaining sea salt.

Preheat the oven to 350°F.

Cover the dough with a dish towel once again, and leave it to rise for another 20 minutes. Then bake in the oven for 25–35 minutes, until pale golden in color and quite soft to the touch. Transfer the focaccia to a wire rack to cool.

Nain's Bara Brith

This is a real Welsh treat. My Nain's recipe for traditional "speckled bread" has been handed down in our family since 1891. We could never go to her house without having a cup of tea and a slice of bara brith. I love to eat it warm, spread generously with salted butter or with a wedge of cheese. And do try it in the Bara Brith Bread and Butter Pudding on page 237.

Dissolve the yeast thoroughly in the lukewarm water.

Mix the flour and the lard together in a large bowl, rubbing the lard into the flour with your fingertips until the texture resembles bread crumbs. Then stir in the sugar, the currants, and the candied peel.

Now pour in the yeast-infused water and mix well until you have a cohesive dough. Turn the dough onto a lightly floured surface and knead it for a good 5 minutes.

Work the bara brith into a long sausage shape to fit the loaf pan. Place it in the lined pan, cover with a dish towel, and leave in a warm place until doubled in size, about an hour or so.

Preheat the oven to 350°F.

Bake the loaf for 40 minutes, or until golden all over. Turn onto a wire rack and set aside to cool.

Makes 1 loaf

½oz fresh yeast

¾ cup lukewarm water

3⅔ cups all-purpose flour, plus extra for dusting

2½oz lard

¼ cup light brown sugar, packed

6oz currants

1oz candied peel, finely sliced

You will need a 2lb loaf pan lined with parchment paper.

Soda Bread

Makes 1 loaf

¾ cup whole wheat flour

¾ cup self-rising flour

1 tbsp baking soda

⅓ cup rolled jumbo oats

¼ cup wheat germ

½ cup wheat bran

2 tsp salt

¼ cup honey

4 tsp molasses

1½ cups buttermilk

You will need a 2lb loaf pan, greased and lined with parchment paper.

This is the easiest of breads—look, no yeast! The loaf is wonderful sliced thickly, then slathered with butter. I also like to serve it with smoked salmon and pickle.

Preheat the oven to 350°F.

Mix all the dry ingredients together in a large bowl and make a well in the center with your fingers.

In a separate bowl, combine the honey, molasses, and buttermilk. Pour the liquid into the well in the flour mixture and, using your fingertips, gradually work them together until they are well incorporated and all the liquid has been absorbed. The mixture should feel runny, almost like a cake mix, so don't worry—you haven't added too much liquid!

Pour the soda-bread mixture into the prepared loaf pan and bake for 40 minutes, until light golden brown. Take it out of the pan immediately and transfer to a wire rack to cool.

BRYN'S TIPS
Always remove bread from the pan immediately and transfer it to a wire rack to cool. If you leave a loaf in the pan it will sweat and become tough.

White Bread Rolls

This basic white bread mix is very similar to the one I made at the bakery all those years ago, and at Odette's we use it to make many kinds of rolls. You could fill the rolls with all manner of things: grainy mustard, poppy seeds, olives, pesto, bacon bits—anything you like; here I've used Spiced Tomato Chutney.

Dissolve the yeast thoroughly in the lukewarm water.

Mix all the dry ingredients together in a large bowl with the olive oil, and make a well in the center with your hands. Then pour in the yeast-infused water.

Using your fingertips, gently and gradually work the flour into the water, until all the liquid has been absorbed and you have a cohesive dough. It should feel smooth, not crumbly or ragged.

Turn the dough onto a well-floured surface and knead it for a good 5 minutes, until it is shiny and smooth and feels silky and elastic.

Place the dough in a clean bowl, cover with a damp dish towel, and leave to rise in a warm place for 30–40 minutes.

When the dough has doubled in size, use your fists to punch down the dough, punching it down into the bowl a couple of times. This removes any air pockets and helps the texture of the bread.

Turn the dough onto a floured surface and roll with a well-floured rolling pin into a rectangular shape. Keep rolling until the dough is about ¼in thick.

Spread the surface of the dough with a good layer of the tomato chutney, then roll it up lengthwise, like a Jelly Roll (see page 223). Roll it as tightly as you can.

Preheat the oven to 350°F.

Cut the dough into 1in slices and place them on a floured baking sheet (you may need two sheets). Cover with a dish towel and leave to rise for 10 minutes, then bake the rolls in the oven for 10–15 minutes, until golden and fragrant. Transfer the rolls immediately to a wire rack to cool. Serve as fresh as possible.

Makes 16–20 rolls

½oz fresh yeast

¾ cup lukewarm water

3½ cups white bread flour, plus extra for dusting

2 tsp salt

2 tsp sugar

2 tsp olive oil

2–3 tsp Spiced Tomato Chutney (see page 252)

Preserves

There was never a time while I was growing up when there wasn't row upon row of gleaming jars on the shelf, filled with a jewel-like array of preserves, chutneys, and pickles. There was something so comforting about them. Something beautiful. And the smell—oh! the smell of fruit and spice, and sugar and vinegar thickening on the stove, tickling your nose and making you salivate just thinking of teatime treats to come. That was my childhood, when all the fruits and vegetables that couldn't be sold or given away were made into precious preserves for the winter months. It's a wonderfully old-fashioned tradition that, now that we can buy certain fruits and vegetables all year round, we have slightly lost touch with. Back in the day, it was the only way to ensure a taste of strawberry or tomatoes in the middle of a long, dark winter.

Preserves and pickles still play a huge part in my cooking. Their depth of flavor and acidity make them perfect accompaniments to savory dishes. And they can be a star in their own right, too, slathered on scones, tarts, jelly rolls, and toast, or propping up cold meats and cheese.

Try using the Lemon Curd here in ice cream, or the Fig Marmalade on a warm croissant. How about pairing the Pear

Chutney with a strong blue cheese and some walnuts, or serving the Spiced Tomato Chutney with cold cuts and savory pies? The uses of these preserves are as endless as the joy you can get from making them.

It's extremely important to sterilize the jars before putting up your preserves. Here's my easy method: wash the jars and lids in warm, soapy water. Rinse them in fresh hot water and set them aside on a dish towel to dry. Then fill a large, deep pan with water and bring it to a boil. Put the jars and lids in the pan and let them simmer for 10 minutes. Remove them with kitchen tongs, making sure that your fingers don't touch the inside of the jars, and set them aside to dry. Or you can put the clean jars and lids into the dishwasher and run it on the hottest cycle without soap. Again, remove everything using tongs and without touching the inside of the jars.

As with many of the dishes in this book, think of the recipes here as guidelines. By adding another spice or using a different sugar you will change the nature and flavor of the recipe and create your own distinctly personal preserves. Before long, your kitchen, too, will contain a gleaming row of homemade preserves.

Pickled Mushrooms

Makes about 2¼lb

2¼lb mushrooms

1¾ cups white wine vinegar

1¼ cups sugar

2 tsp sea salt

1 garlic clove, peeled
and crushed

1 red chile, split (if the chile
is hot you can deseed it)

sprig of thyme

1 bay leaf

You will need sterilized
preserving jars with lids
(see page 245).

These little beauties can enliven so many dishes. Scatter a few into Mushroom Soup (see page 36) and enjoy the way the tart pickle plays against the soup's earthy creaminess, or nestle a generous spoonful next to a game terrine or some smoked meats. You can use any mushrooms you like—I've used buttons and criminis to great effect.

Wash and dry the mushrooms, then place them in a pan with a snug-fitting lid.

Put the vinegar, sugar, salt, crushed garlic, and chile in a pan over medium heat, bring to a boil, and allow to simmer for 2 minutes, then add the thyme and bay leaf. Pour the mixture over the mushrooms, put the lid on the pan immediately, and set aside to cool.

Divide the mushrooms and preserving liquid between clean, sterilized jars and seal. Label the jars with the date so you can keep track of different batches. Leave to cool and refrigerate. If you can bear to, leave them a week or two before opening. They will keep for up to 6 months in the fridge.

Lemon Curd

Luscious, lemony, and creamy, this curd is perfect on hot buttered toast or to fill sweet tarts for a teatime treat. It's also fantastic with sharp, crumbly cheeses, and makes a great filling for the Jelly Roll on page 223.

Put the lemon juice, butter, and sugar in a heatproof bowl over a saucepan of barely simmering water, making sure the water does not touch the bowl. Stir until the butter has melted and the sugar has dissolved.

Add the beaten eggs and cook gently, whisking occasionally, until the mixture thickens. It should coat the back of a spoon.

Divide between clean, sterilized jars while still warm, and seal. Label the jars with the date so you can keep track of different batches. Leave to cool, then refrigerate. This will keep for up to 2 weeks in the refrigerator.

Makes about 2 cups

juice of 4 lemons

½ cup unsalted butter, cut into cubes

1½ cups sugar

4 eggs, beaten

You will need sterilized preserving jars with lids (see page 245).

Pear Chutney

Makes about 2lb

2½ cups superfine sugar

1¾ cups white wine vinegar

9oz chopped onion

juice of 2 oranges

1 tsp salt

½ tsp cayenne pepper

½ tsp ground ginger

1 tsp ground cinnamon

1 tsp grated nutmeg

4½lb pears, peeled, cored, and chopped

9oz golden raisins

You will need sterilized preserving jars with lids (see page 245).

The sweetness of the pears and the gentle warmth of the spices make this chutney a real treat. Pair it with the rich Chicken Liver Pâté on page 120 or the Game Terrine on page 162. You could also try it with cheeses and smoked meats.

Put all the ingredients except the pears and the golden raisins into a large, heavy-bottomed saucepan. Bring to a boil. Reduce the heat and simmer, stirring from time to time, until the mixture has a jamlike consistency—this will take about 5 minutes.

Add the chopped pears and cook for 20 minutes, then add the golden raisins and mix through. Remove from the heat.

Divide between clean, sterilized jars and seal. Label the jars with the date so you can keep track of different batches. Leave to cool, then refrigerate. This will keep for up to 6 months in the fridge.

Spiced Tomato Chutney

Makes about 2 cups

½ cup malt vinegar

1 cup light brown sugar

2 tbsp tomato paste

2 tsp salt

1 tsp chile powder

1 tsp ground ginger

2¼lb plum tomatoes, skinned, deseeded, and roughly chopped

You will need sterilized preserving jars with lids (see page 245).

With its hits of chile and ginger, this tomato chutney packs a punch. It's amazing with cheese and makes a great accompaniment to lamb. I sometimes stir some into lamb stews and tagines, and the flavors marry beautifully.

Put the vinegar, sugar, tomato paste, salt, chile powder, and ground ginger into a heavy-bottomed pan and bring to a boil. Add the chopped tomatoes and simmer very gently for 30–40 minutes, stirring occasionally to prevent it from sticking, until the mixture thickens and has a jamlike consistency.

Divide the chutney between clean, sterilized jars. Label the jars with the date so you can keep track of different batches. Leave to cool, then refrigerate. This will keep in the fridge for up to 6 months.

Fig Marmalade

This is like sending your taste buds along the Spice Route. It's gorgeous with the Wood Pigeon on page 169, but you could also try it on toast in the morning, or with some strong blue cheese.

Lightly crush the peppercorns, juniper berries, and cardamom pods and tie them up in a small piece of muslin or clean cloth to make a spice bag. Set aside.

Put the figs in a pan with the lemon juice, orange juice, white wine, sugar, and honey. Bring to a boil. Add the lemon zest, the orange zest, and the spice bag, then reduce the heat to medium-low and let the mixture cook, stirring occasionally, until it has a thick, jamlike consistency, about 15 minutes.

Remove the zest and the spice bag, then transfer the marmalade to a clean, sterilized jar and seal. Label with the date so you can keep track of different batches. Leave to cool, then refrigerate. This will keep for up to 6 months in the fridge.

Makes about 1 cup

4 peppercorns

4 juniper berries

2 cardamom pods

14 fresh figs, roughly chopped

juice and thinly pared zest of 2 lemons

juice and thinly pared zest of 2 oranges

4 tbsp white wine

4 tbsp sugar

1 tbsp honey

You will need a sterilized preserving jar with a lid (see page 245).

Stocks

I feel that recipes and the way in which you execute them are an expression of yourself: they present your personality on a plate. And the basic tools you need to create them are handed down from chef to chef, and in families from generation to generation.

Stocks are one of the building blocks of tasty, memorable dishes. How many sauces, risottos, soups, ragouts, stews, and braises have these simple amalgamations of trimmings and water at their core? By using a good stock, you immediately add a base of flavor and body to a dish—before you've even gathered together any other ingredients. And having a stock or two under your belt gives you the foundation you need to expand your repertoire of dishes. Stocks are also a simple and staggeringly tasty example of my "no waste" philosophy.

I'm not going to frown if you use a good-quality, ready-made stock. But I do urge you to try out these recipes. They really take no time at all, happily humming away on the stove while you get on with something else. They make the kitchen smell amazing. And, above all, they make a huge difference to the flavor of your finished dishes.

Mushroom Stock

Makes about 2 cups

1 tbsp vegetable oil

1 onion, peeled and thinly sliced

18oz wild mushroom trimmings, washed

2 garlic cloves, peeled and crushed

sprig of thyme

sprig of rosemary

⅓ cup Madeira

2½ cups water

When you cook with wild mushrooms, there are always some trimmings left over. This is a great way of using them up and not wasting anything. Use this stock as a base for Mushroom Soup (see page 36) and Mushroom Risotto (see page 34) or for earthy soups and gravies.

In a heavy-bottomed saucepan, heat the oil, then add the onion and cook until golden. Add the mushroom trimmings, the crushed garlic, thyme, and rosemary, and cook for another 5 minutes, until almost dry.

Pour in the Madeira and let it reduce to a syrup. Add the water, bring to a boil, and allow to simmer for 5 minutes.

Pass the stock through a fine strainer and cool it as quickly as possible. This will keep for up to 3 days in the fridge. It also freezes well.

Vegetable Stock

So useful and so simple, this is the base I rely on for a multitude of soups, including the Leek & Potato Soup on page 42. Start by chopping all the vegetables into uniform pieces, about ¹/₂in or so in size. Then they will cook evenly and maximize the flavor of the stock.

Bring the water and wine to a boil in a large, heavy-bottomed saucepan. Add all the chopped vegetables, the herbs and spices, and the salt and pepper, then let the pan simmer gently for 10 minutes, until the vegetables are just cooked but still have some bite.

Remove the pan from the heat and allow it to cool naturally, leaving the vegetables in the stock.

Strain the stock and refrigerate until needed. This will keep for up to 3 days in the fridge. It also freezes well.

Makes about 1 quart

1½ quarts water

²⁄₃ cup white wine

2 carrots, peeled and chopped

2 shallots, peeled and chopped

1 celery stick, chopped

1 small leek, chopped

2 bay leaves

8 peppercorns

1 tsp fennel seeds

2 star anise

2 tsp celery salt

salt and pepper

Fish Stock

Fish stock makes a wonderful base for seafood soups, stews, and sauces. Your local fishmonger will be more than happy to supply the bones.

Rinse the fish bones under cold water, then set them aside to dry on paper towels before starting the stock.

In a heavy-bottomed saucepan, heat the olive oil and cook the onion, celery and leek until soft, without letting them color.

Add the fish bones, stir well to combine them with the vegetables and cook for another 1–2 minutes. Pour in the wine and let it boil for another minute, then add enough cold water just to cover the fish bones. If you add too much water you will dilute the flavor. Bring it back to a boil over high heat, then reduce the heat so that the stock just simmers. Skim off any fat that rises to the surface.

Add the bay leaves, peppercorns, and lemon slices to the saucepan and continue simmering gently for 20 minutes, without letting it boil, skimming off fat whenever necessary.

Pass the stock through a fine strainer and cool it as quickly as possible. This stock will keep for up to 3 days in the fridge. It also freezes well.

Makes 1¹/₂–2 quarts

3½lb fish bones, roughly chopped

3 tbsp olive oil

1 onion, peeled and thinly sliced

1 celery stick, finely sliced

1 small leek, finely sliced

¹⁄₃ cup white wine

2 bay leaves

8 peppercorns

2 slices of lemon

Smoked Salmon Stock

If you ever have a side of smoked salmon, try this stock. It's a great way to use up all the little trimmings—even the skin and bones—you have left over. You can also buy the trimmings from the supermarket or deli, which makes this an economical stock that tastes expensive. Add a dash of cream to create a delicious cream of smoked salmon soup, or serve it clear, as a consommé, with a few diced spring vegetables. You can also use this to make the Smoked Salmon Risotto on page 82.

In a heavy-bottomed saucepan, heat the olive oil over low heat and cook the onion, celery, leek, and fennel until soft, without letting them color. Add the tomato paste and cook for 1 minute.

Add the smoked salmon trimmings, cover with water, and bring to a boil over high heat, then reduce to a simmer. Skim off any fat that rises to the surface. Add the bay leaves, peppercorns, and star anise and gently simmer for 10 minutes, without boiling, skimming off the fat whenever necessary.

Pass the stock through a fine strainer and cool it as quickly as possible. This will keep for up to 3 days in the fridge. It also freezes well.

Makes about 1 quart

3 tbsp olive oil

1 onion, peeled and thinly sliced

1 celery stick, trimmed and finely chopped

1 small leek, trimmed and thinly sliced

1 small fennel bulb, trimmed and finely chopped

2 tbsp tomato paste

18oz smoked salmon trimmings

2 bay leaves

8 peppercorns

1 star anise

Chicken Stock

This stock is the basis of so many of my dishes and, like most of the other stocks in this chapter, is not hard to make. You can use it for a quick soup, too. Just boil up some chicken, add some chunky vegetables and there you go—delicious.

Put the chicken bones in a large, heavy-bottomed saucepan and add just enough cold water to cover the bones. Don't add too much water or you will reduce the flavor of the stock.

Bring the pan to a boil over high heat, then reduce the heat to a simmer. Skim off any fat or foamy scum that rises to the surface. Add all the chopped vegetables and herbs to the pan and allow to simmer gently for 2 hours, without boiling. Skim off any scum or any fat that rises to the surface.

Pass the stock through a fine strainer and cool it as quickly as possible. This will keep for up to 3 days in the fridge. It also freezes well.

Makes 1.5–2 quarts

3½lb raw chicken bones or 1–2 cooked carcasses from a roast (see tips, below)

1 onion, peeled and coarsely chopped

1 celery stick, trimmed and coarsely chopped

1 small leek, trimmed and coarsely chopped

2 bay leaves

2 sprigs of thyme

BRYN'S TIPS
Raw chicken bones give a lot of flavor—ask your butcher for them. If you can't get them, just use the bones from your last roast, and don't cook the stock as long—about 1 hour will do.

If one roast chicken carcass doesn't provide enough bones, freeze it. Wait to make the stock until you have enough frozen carcasses. Then just thaw them out when you're ready to cook.

Savory Sauces

A good dish is not just about taste; it's about balance and texture. Sauces exist to enhance these aspects of our cooking. They don't just add a bit of liquid to the plate, but instead bring everything together, contributing moisture, flavor, and contrast to raise the feel of a recipe. I would never serve a piece of fish without a squeeze of lemon juice, because that extra dash of acidity brings out all the fish's natural layers of flavor. Sauces have a similar effect. Take a great piece of steak, for example, cook it simply, then add a spiky pepper sauce. Suddenly it's transformed into the best steak in the world.

Sometimes, sauce-making can seem a bit too "cheffy" and difficult, but the simplest sauces are very easy—like adding some wine to a roasting pan and scraping up the sticky pieces the roast has left behind. So, aside from the Hollandaise on page 261, I've tried to keep the sauces in this chapter pretty straightforward. I make all five of them all the time.

You'll always find a bottle of the Ketchup in my fridge, and whenever my family roasts a chicken or a game bird, I have to make the Bread Sauce—they'd never let me get away with it if I didn't! The Curried Fruit Sauce comes from my time working at Le Gavroche, and always evokes happy memories of the early days of my career. I find the Creamed Fish Sauce adds a richness to any steamed, poached, or broiled fish, particularly sole. And as for the Hollandaise Sauce, well, that takes a bit of effort, but, trust me, the results are worth it. I love the way it lifts so many things, from a perfect piece of fish to a classic brunch-time eggs Benedict. And, particularly with some freshly steamed asparagus, it's the king of sauces.

Creamed Fish Sauce

Makes about 1½ cups

¼ cup unsalted butter

1 shallot, peeled and thinly sliced

5 button mushrooms, thinly sliced

1 bay leaf

⅓ cup white wine

1 cup Fish Stock (see page 257)

1 cup heavy cream

salt and pepper

1 lemon

This just goes to show what a rich and sophisticated sauce you can make from pantry basics, fish stock, and some cream. It's perfect with steamed or poached fish, such as sole, halibut, or salmon. It's a great sauce to have in your repertoire because it's also the base for so many variations. You can add chopped chives, brown shrimp, or any number of different mustards to charge it up.

In a heavy-bottomed saucepan, melt the butter and cook the shallot until soft, without letting it color. Add the mushrooms and the bay leaf and cook for another 2–3 minutes. Again, don't let the shallot catch any color. Pour in the white wine, bring to a boil, and let it bubble away until the volume is reduced by half.

Add the fish stock, bring back to a boil, and again reduce the liquid by half. Add the heavy cream and bring to a simmer for 6–7 minutes, until the sauce thickens.

Pass the sauce through a fine strainer, season with salt and pepper, and finish with a squeeze of lemon juice. Serve hot over, or on the side of, fish. Once cooled, this sauce will keep in the fridge for up to 3 days.

Curried Fruit Sauce

Sweet and spicy at the same time, this sauce is simple to make and an easy way to brighten up broiled or barbecued fish and meats. Whenever I had to make this I was always sure I got the leftovers—I'd eat it every day. I particularly like it with pork chops: it lifts them to a new level.

Melt the butter in a heavy-bottomed saucepan. Add the shallot and cook for about 1 minute, without letting it color. Add the chopped pineapple, banana, and apple and gently cook until soft, 4–5 minutes.

Add the curry powder and cook for another minute. Pour in the chicken stock and the coconut milk, bring back to a boil, and simmer for 10–15 minutes.

To finish the sauce, process it in a blender or food processor, then pass through a fine strainer. Serve hot with the meat, fish, or vegetables of your choice. Once cooled, this sauce will keep in the fridge, covered, for up to 3 days.

Serves 4–6

2½ tbsp unsalted butter

1 shallot, peeled and finely chopped

9oz pineapple, peeled, cored, and chopped

1 banana, peeled and chopped

1 apple, peeled, cored, and chopped

5½ tbsp curry powder

1¾ cups Chicken Stock (see page 259)

⅔ cup coconut milk

Hollandaise Sauce

Perfect for eggs Benedict or to serve on the side of a broiled piece of fish, this classic sauce goes beautifully with steamed asparagus, too. My particular favorite way of serving it is with steak. It can be a bit complicated and takes some practice, but once you've got it down, it's easy, and you'll make it time and time again.

In a saucepan, bring the vinegar, peppercorns, thyme, and bay leaf to a boil, and simmer until the liquid is reduced by half. Don't worry if this seems like a lot of vinegar—you will need only a little. Keep the rest in the fridge, covered, for up to 6 months.

Melt the butter in a saucepan over low heat until it starts to foam. Spoon off the foam and discard. Leave the remaining butter to settle. Remove the clarified butter—the clear yellow liquid left in the pan after you have skimmed off the foam—with a ladle and then discard the white residue remaining at the bottom of the pan.

Place the egg yolks and 2 tablespoons of the reduced vinegar in a heatproof bowl over a saucepan of barely simmering water. Make sure that the water does not touch the bowl—if it does, the mixture will get too hot and scramble the eggs. Whisk the egg yolk mixture until it is light and creamy.

Remove the bowl from the heat, whisking continuously, and gently pour in the clarified butter. Pass the mixture through a fine strainer, then season to taste with salt and pepper and a squeeze of lemon juice. Serve immediately.

Serves 4–6

⅔ cup white wine vinegar

10 peppercorns, crushed

sprig of thyme

1 bay leaf

1 cup unsalted butter

5 egg yolks

salt and pepper

1 lemon

Bread Sauce

Serves 4–6

6 slices of thick white bread

1 onion, peeled and cut in half

1 bay leaf

1 clove

1¾ cups milk

¼ cup butter

salt and pepper

pinch of grated nutmeg

No one can beat my Mam's Christmas dinner—I would never even dare try—but my one job on the day is to make this bread sauce. It's a must-have with all game and bird dishes. This is based on my Nain's recipe. She would use bread crumbs, but I prefer fresh chunks of thick white bread.

Cut the crusts off the bread and discard. Then cut the slices into 1in squares. Chop one half of the onion as finely as you can and leave the other half intact.

Place the intact onion half, bay leaf, and clove in a small saucepan with the milk and bring to a boil. Simmer gently for about 2 minutes. Take off the heat and set aside to cool.

In a heavy-bottomed pan, melt the butter and sauté the chopped onion. Cook the onion gently, until it is soft but not colored, about 2 minutes.

Pass the milk through a sieve and pour it onto the sautéed onion. Now bring this to a boil. Once it reaches boiling point, remove from the heat and add the bread. Stir until everything is combined and slightly softened—it should retain some texture. Season with salt, pepper, and nutmeg. Cover the pan with a lid and keep warm until needed.

Ketchup

Makes just under 2 cups

¾ cup malt vinegar

½ cup demerara sugar

3½lb ripe tomatoes, deseeded and chopped

1 shallot, peeled and finely chopped

½ tsp ground cinnamon

½ tsp ground coriander

½ tsp sea salt

2 garlic cloves, peeled and finely chopped

2oz tomato paste

You will need sterilized preserving jars with lids (see page 245).

What could be better than homemade ketchup? And this sauce is so very simple to make. Trust me: everybody loves it, and it will get used up before you know it. I always have a bottle of it in my fridge at home. So give it a try. You'll find yourself making it time and again, whether it's for the Bacon & Tomato Sandwich on page 151 or to be squirted liberally onto anything you choose.

Put the vinegar and the sugar in a heavy-bottomed saucepan, and bring it to a boil over medium heat, stirring while the sugar dissolves. Add the chopped tomatoes, followed by all the other ingredients. Bring back to a boil, stirring occasionally, then simmer for 40 minutes. Take the pan off the heat and allow it to cool slightly.

Process the mixture in a blender or food processor, then pass it through a fine strainer, pressing hard to get all those precious juices out.

Return the sauce to a clean saucepan and bring it back to a boil. Check the consistency—it should be thick and unctuous by now. Take the pan off the heat and pour the ketchup into clean, sterilized jars, then seal them. Label the jars with the date so you can keep track of different batches. Leave to cool, then refrigerate. This will keep for up to 4–6 weeks in the fridge.

Sweet Sauces

Everybody loves dessert, but so often you want something extra to go with it, to give a it that added oomph. Maybe because dessert comes at the end of the meal, it's easy to forget about the finishing touches and default to cream or ice cream as an accompaniment to so many crumbles and pies.

With this section, I'm setting out to make amends. These basic recipes for sweet sauces will transform your desserts. They're all quite simple to follow, they taste great, and, what's more, look really impressive at the end of a meal.

Who doesn't love to drown their crumble in custard? My plate is certainly always overflowing. So here's a Vanilla Custard that beats any ice-cream-on-the-side hands down. There's a rich Chocolate Sauce that goes brilliantly with, well, ice cream. I absolutely love butterscotch, so I had to include a Butterscotch Sauce here—this one is redolent of childhood memories; the smell alone takes me back in time. The Caramel Sauce adds an extra, darkly sweet zing to any steamed or baked dessert, while the Brandy Sauce is a bit more grown up, and no less delicious for it. To me, this sauce just yells "Christmas!" Try one of these treats next time you make dessert, for an extra-sweet ending to the meal.

Chocolate Sauce

Serves 4

¾ cup water

7 tbsp superfine sugar

⅔ cup cocoa powder

3½oz good-quality dark chocolate, minimum 70 percent cocoa solids, roughly chopped

¼ cup unsalted butter, cut into small pieces

This is deliciously chocolatey and goes beautifully with ice cream as well as with the Chocolate Sponge Cake on page 200. You could also pour it over a pile of profiteroles. Kids just love it.

In a large, heavy-bottomed saucepan, bring the water, the sugar, and the cocoa to a boil. Remove from the heat immediately.

Add the chopped chocolate and the butter to the saucepan and whisk everything until it comes together.

Pass the sauce through a fine strainer and pour into a clean pitcher or bowl. Serve either hot or cold.

Brandy Sauce

I serve this every year with Christmas pudding, but it's good with the Chocolate Sponge Cake on page 200, too—and it also works, quite frankly, just with a spoon.

In a small bowl, mix 2 tablespoons of the milk with the cornstarch to make a paste.

Bring the rest of the milk and the cream to a boil in a heavy-bottomed saucepan, then whisk in the cornstarch paste. Bring back to a boil.

Add the butter, sugar, and brandy and mix well. This is a thin, pouring sauce, so don't allow it to get too thick. When you are happy with the consistency, place a lid on the saucepan to prevent the sauce from developing a skin, set aside, and keep warm until needed.

Serves 4–6

¾ cup milk

1 tsp cornstarch

¾ cup heavy cream

2 tbsp butter

2½ tbsp superfine sugar

3 tbsp brandy

Butterscotch Sauce

This is one of those sauces that everyone loves, but no one knows how to make. It's so simple. I like to marry this old-fashioned-tasting sauce with the Baked Apples on page 176.

Gently melt the sugar in a heavy-bottomed saucepan over low to medium heat until it turns a dark caramel color. Remove from the heat immediately.

Pour in the cream—the pan will spit, so stand back—and whisk continuously. Once all the cream has been incorporated, add the butter, whisking that in, too. Serve warm.

Serves 4–6

1½ cups superfine sugar

⅔ cup heavy cream

1½ cups unsalted butter, cut into small pieces

Vanilla Custard

Serves 4

8 egg yolks

½ cup superfine sugar

1 cup milk

⅔ cup heavy cream

1 vanilla pod, split in half
and seeds scraped out

As far as my dad's concerned, if something's got custard, he's right in there. So I had to include this classic, old-fashioned Vanilla Custard in the book. Sweet pies and crumbles were invented for it. So you know: Dad also feels that custard must come to the table in its own pitcher. That way, you can make sure you get plenty!

In a large bowl, whisk the egg yolks and the sugar together until thick and creamy.

Bring the milk and the cream to simmer in a heavy-bottomed saucepan with the vanilla pod and seeds. Take the pan off the heat and pour the hot milk onto the egg-yolk mixture, whisking continuously.

Pour the mixture back into the saucepan and cook over low heat, stirring continuously with a spatula or a wooden spoon, until the custard thickens enough to coat the back of the spoon.

Pass the custard through a fine strainer and serve hot.

Caramel Sauce

Serves 4

1½ cups superfine sugar

1 cup heavy cream

Here we have a great, sticky, caramelly sauce that is wonderful with the Apple Tarte Tatin on page 181 as an alternative to the Calvados Cream. Try it also with ice cream or drizzled over baked bananas. Both this and the Butterscotch Sauce on page 265 are really quick to make. One pan, one whisk, and, in both cases, you've got a great sauce.

Gently melt the sugar in a heavy-bottomed saucepan over medium heat, until it turns a dark caramel color. Remove from the heat immediately.

Pour in the cream, whisking continuously. The cream will start to spit because of the heat, but don't worry, just keep on whisking until all the cream is incorporated. Leave to cool before serving.

Index

Acknowledgments

It goes without saying that every book has a team behind it, and if weren't for Kay this book would not have been possible because no one could read the bloody recipes. Also Kay, thanks for capturing me and putting me down on paper, some would say an impossible job, but you made it look easy.

Gordon, thanks for seeing the vision of the book, for making it possible and for listening to my rants over the phone day and night.

Thanks to Kyle Cathie for believing in me and the book, and to Jenny for pulling it all together.

Jonathan: mouth-watering photography always makes a cookbook special.
Thank you for the most amazing photos and for capturing my food the way I imagined it. Thanks, too, to Tamin: a much appreciated second eye on the photo shoots.

To have amazing photography, you need amazing-looking food: Annie, what a great cook you are and you make it look so easy. Rachel, thanks for all the help you gave—it goes to show that too many cooks don't spoil the broth.

Liz: a big thanks for hunting high and low to find the props that pulled everything together. It looks fantastic.

The design of this book comes down to Alan and Lisa at Aboud Creative. Thanks for the vision and direction you both brought to the book, and as always, Alan, you bring something special out of that bag of yours. It's absolutely amazing.

Thanks to Poku and the team at Odette's for holding it all together while the book was being written, and to Ana for juggling the dates.

Food's all about sharing, so I want to thank my family for all the picnics we've had and my friends for all the times we have shared around the table.

Diolch Mam, Dad, Gareth a Sion.

Nain, Diolch am y Bara Brith.